Germany East and West

Germany East and West

Conflicts, Collaboration, and Confrontation

Lawrence L. Whetten

New York University Press • New York *and* London

Copyright © 1980 by New York University

Library of Congress Cataloging in Publication Data

Whetten, Lawrence L
  Germany East and West.

  Includes bibliographical references and index.
  1. Germany, West—Foreign relations—Germany, East.
2. Germany, East—Foreign relations—Germany, West.
3. Germany, West—Foreign relations—Europe, Eastern.
4. Europe, Eastern—Foreign relations—Germany, West.
5. World politics—1945–   I. Title.
DD259.4.W438   327.430431   79-3713
ISBN 0-8147-9193-X

Manufactured in the United States of America

To Hildegard Indra

Acknowledgements

I wish to express my appreciation to the management and staff of the Federal Ministry for Inner German Relations for valuable assistance in compiling some of the statistical data, especially, Ministerialdirigent Dr. Hansjürgen Schierbaum und Dr. Joseph Dolezal.

My gratitude should also be expressed to the Council of Foreign Relations, New York, for originally sponsoring the project and to Robert G. Livingston, President, German Marshall, who painstakingly read an initial draft and offered invaluable insights. I have also been fortunate to be surrounded by German colleagues with rich depths in experience that have been indispensable in analyzing the range of issues contained in this short book.

I am also grateful for the valuable research assistance provided by my wife, Gabriele.

Contents

Introduction

There are several basic factors that have influenced relations between the two Germanys over the past quarter century. Some factors the two sides have shared in common, some have had the centripetal effect of enhancing their mutual bonds and still others have nurtured separatist tendencies and parochial distinctiveness.[1]

Whether one accepts the formula of the Federal Republic of Germany, of two states in one nation, or the prescription of the German Democratic Republic, of two separate and equal states, both entities share a common cultural and social background which continues to influence national policy and public behavior. The common language and history are strong bonds that cannot be dismissed. Varying interpretations of Goethe, Schiller, and Brecht or of the causes of World War II and German war guilt have not yet nullified their common origins. Indeed, discussions of these interpretations frequently reinforce this joint heritage. As the urgency to reunite has receded on both sides, increased emphasis on the Germanic background of both parts seem to emerge as an inevitable consequence. True, the GDR has been more reluctant for political reasons to acknowledge its legacy. But as formal FRG recognition of its statehood have begun to bear practical results, fears that mutual links to the past would permeate unduly the partition have gradually declined.

Both states have other factors in common. They share similar geostrategic positions. With a common border, they are exposed on the front line of the East-West confrontation. Each has impressive armed forces (the Bundeswehr is the largest and best-trained army in Western Europe and the Nationale Volksarmee is probably the best-disciplined East European force). Yet both have explicit limitations imposed on their military

strength; that is, neither state can acquire strategic capabilities
nor significantly increase the size of its armed forces. Furthermore, both sides trade moderately with each other, and access
to West German technology and to modest amounts of interest-
free credits have provided distinct advantages for the GDR.
Thus, they have parallel postures in their respective alliances:
They rank number two in economic and political power in both
security systems, and each has served as the prime mover in
the integration of their respective halves of Europe. Most
remarkable from the perspective of historical European antece-
dents, these achievements were accomplished despite, and
possibly because of, the constraints placed on the armaments
and military capabilities of both German states by the presence
of foreign troops on their respective territories.

There are also tendencies in both states and both alliances
that encourage separateness and distinctive national development. Traditional sectional traits persist and tend to reinforce
the political systems on both sides: The austere, puritanical,
moralistic and group-oriented Prussians and Saxons regard the
Rheinlanders and Bavarians as undisciplined and individualis-
tic. Such amorphic features tend to support the respective
forms of government adopted by each side, the one authoritarian and the other democratic. True the East Germans have
been able to foster a form of national communism, especially in
the economy, that is not identical with the other brands of
Socialist development, and the West Germans have evolved a
hybrid of social democracy that has few identical parallels in
the Western world. But the two respective models for social
progress are both sufficiently unique and divergent that the
possibility of convergence and the establishment of common
institutions is indeed remote.

As the main economic and political focal points in central
Europe of both alliances, the two Germanys are respected and
possibly envied by their allies and rivals. Nonetheless, there is
little sympathy in either pact for sponsorship of German reunification. Indeed, genuine movement toward the formation of a
greater Germany would trigger sharp negative reactions among
virtually all members of both alliances. Indeed the "German

problem" for both regions has now become the question of how to harness the political and economic energies and ambitions of the two separate Germanys. Yet, the basic factors governing contemporary relations between the FRG and GDR may be characterized as divergent pursuits of individual national aims. The Federal Republic finally has accepted the proposition that, over time, the pursuit of their respective national identities will gradually strengthen the mutual ties between neighboring states with a common history, that is, reunification—a mandate of the FRG Constitution—through mutual accommodation of respective state's interests. The Democratic Republic, in contrast, is more defensive and less flexible. Legitimization of the rule of the Sozialistische Einheitspartei Deutschlands (SED) is the immediate reason for promoting East German national character. The long-range objective is the ultimate socialization of greater Germany—a basic premise of the original GDR Constitution. Thus, the constitutional tenets of both Germanys and the evolution of their relations suggest at this juncture the possibility both of adjustment and subsequent identification of "greater Germanic interests" and of confrontation and continued inner German tensions. Both eventualities would be the subject of international concern.

The partial conciliation between 1972 and 1978 produced agonizing individual and collective soul-searching. Chancellor Adenauer, as Stresemann in 1925, sought to rectify German war guilt and restore national dignity through integration and solidarity with the West, while keeping German options open in the East. Traditionally Germans have concluded that the best barometer of their stature as a world power has not been the establishment of overseas colonies or a confrontation with the Western powers, but rather the exercise of control or hegemony over various East European entities. The West was the chief threat; the East the land of opportunities. Thus, for Adenauer, gaining respectability in the West through demonstrating responsibility was intended to refurbish German national prestige and enhance the prospects for achieving reunification on Bonn's terms of self-determination and the establishment of common institutions by insuring that Bonn could deal from a position of strength. The policy was only partially successful: Integration in the West contributed to the "economic miracle" and the return to prosperity in the FRG, but it failed to achieve reunification.[2]

The construction of the Berlin Wall in August 1961 was a sharp blow against West German foreign policy. No other single event was as significant in forcing the reappraisal of Bonn's general Eastern policy. Over several years, the Social Democratic party (SPD) gradually recognized that a modified stand toward the GDR might provide both political leverage against the entrenched Christian Democratic party (CDU) and improve the lot of East German citizens. This awareness brought about decisions that finally created the atmosphere conducive for the negotiations of the treaties now collectively known as the *Ostverträge*. Events that led to the change in the West German attitude toward Eastern Europe in general, and the GDR in particular, will be traced in four main areas: relations between German Socialists and Communists, the evolution of West German politics, interactions of East Germany and Rumania on the German problem, and negotiations between East and West Germany.

Chapter I

Early FRG-GDR Relations

GERMAN SOCIALISTS AND COMMUNISTS

Since the initiative to modify Bonn's Eastern policy had its roots in earlier decisions that had nearly destroyed the Social Democratic party and reduced it to its lowest political ebb, it is appropriate to examine its previous relations with the Communists for indications of the motivations and intentions behind the SPD's move. The bitter disputes that erupted among Socialists on the proper relations to be maintained with the Communists created deep ideological and political chasms that had to be overcome before a dialogue and possible reconciliation with the GDR was conceivable.[3] The CDU position on reunification was well known, and, in order to provide either a viable alternative or a national consensus with the CDU, the Socialists first had to reconcile themselves with their legacy of complicity with the Communists in attempting to establish a socialist state after World War II.

During the interwar years the Social Democrats represented the majority of the leftist sentiment and were labelled the main class enemy by the German Communist party (KPD) and the Soviets through the Comintern. After Hitler's ascendancy to power, a minority of the KPD Central Committee, including Wilhelm Pieck and Walter Ulbricht, followed the experiment of the French Communists and advocated as early as the fall of 1934 a policy reversal, embracing full collaboration with the Socialists. The SPD leadership rejected the offer on the grounds that the Nazis could then claim that their only enemy

[1]

was Bolshevism. The SPD in general continued to reject collaboration through the war because of the Soviet party purges, the August 1939 Soviet-German Treaty and the gradual disintegration of the SPD through imprisonment and exile. Anxieties about earlier SPD relations with the Communists and the nature of future contacts led to bitter infighting and factionalism among the Socialists as soon as the war ended.[4]

The Socialists' postwar plans were as scattered as were their dislocated leaders. The most radical proposals were made by individuals imprisoned together with Communists and the more moderate by those exiled in Switzerland and Britain. In general, however, Socialists of all stripes were prepared to do penance and pay a heavy penalty for their failure to cooperate more fully with the Communists during the Hitler era.[5] An SPD Manifesto in April 1945, for example, demanded dissolution of formal political parties, government by People's Committees, foreign policy coordination with the USSR, extension of socialism from Eastern Europe to all Europe, and adoption of the Leninist principle of democratic centralism: "Freedom in discussion, discipline in execution." Individual SPD bodies rejected the Manifesto but retained portions of its contents.[6]

The SPD began organizing itself at three specific levels. A Central Committee was established in Berlin with authority in the Soviet Zone after the fall of the Reich. The party established *Initiativgruppen* in each provincial capital, headed by a member of the Politburo or Central Committee, but staffed by Thus prominent socialist personalities created power bases at various planes and vied with each other over ideological principles and party leadership. The Soviets attempted to organize both the SPD and the CDU on a nationwide scale as possible bases for the extension of Soviet influence into other zones, and encouraged the SPD Central Committee to convene a legitimizing party congress on June 17, 1945, that would confirm the leadership and establish party policy. But less than one fifth of the 1700 delegates came from the more numerous Western SPD bodies, thus undermining the Central Committee's authority from the outset and directing Soviet attention back to zonal political developments.

Before the Party Congress the Central Committee issued its first proclamation proposing a more moderate stand than it had in earlier documents, which it hoped would gain universal acclamation by the Congress. It advocated democracy in government, socialism in the economy, organizational integrity of the working class and the immediate unification of the socialist and communist parties. The socialist delegates to the Congress accepted the call for unity, but the Communists rejected the offer outright.

The KPD would not dissolve itself and maintained that it was the vanguard of the workers' movement. It continually charged that the SPD failures during the 1930s were the result of its rejection of communist partnership. The SPD leadership in general saw earlier errors as the product of mutual hostilities between the two parties and mistakenly presumed that the KPD shared its desire to make a clean break with the disastrous past by opening a new era based upon mutual dissolution and unity of the working class.[7]

These misperceptions were partially understandable. After all, Communist party members were performing in a responsible manner in as many as nine Western governments, notably in France and Italy, and the KPD was most energetic in seizing and organizing the state administrative machinery throughout the Soviet Zone after the fall of the Reich. The party established *Initiativgruppen* in each provincial capital, headed by a member of the Politburo or Central Committee, but staffed by leftists. Some were opportunists, but many were SPD members. A deliberate effort was made to portray the image of genuine coalition in state administration. Yet, it was precisely this impression of coalition politics that allowed the KPD to reject unity. The new machinery lacked adequate centralized control and discipline. Ulbricht asserted, "We must learn to lead the millions, to lead the masses step by step. . . . We cannot establish a Soviet system with submachine guns. . . . The KPD must strengthen itself and fortify itself ideologically . . . and prove itself to the masses through its work in responsible administration."[8] Throughout the summer and fall of 1945, the KPD continued to turn down the Socialists' call for immediate unity before adequate ideological purification had occurred. Ulbricht insisted ambiguously that "democracy not socialism is the immediate problem," which, in communist terms, meant the thorough imposition of democratic centralism.

The failure of the Congress that had been called to legitimize the SPD soon had adverse implications for the Committee's attempt to consolidate its authority, even within the Soviet Zone, by underscoring its inability to centralize control over *Bezirk* leaders and establish a common policy position. The difficulties in consolidating its position were due to the relatively junior stature of its leaders, Allied interzonal politics, effective resistance by Western SPD bodies to the Committee's overtures, and the obvious interference in SPD affairs at the local level by the Soviet Military Authority (SMA) and the KPD. Lacking effective centralization and Soviet patronage, the Central Committee soon felt outmaneuvered at the levels of the *Bezirk* party committees and state administration.

Yet it was at this juncture (during August and September 1945), and partially for these reasons, that the popularity of the SPD rose sharply and that of the KPD began to fall, especially in factory elections. SMA and KPD policy was faced with a fundamental problem: The strategic aim of organizing "progressive" political forces throughout Germany and possibly Europe was jeopardized for the first time by the tactical question of defusing the rising popularity of the socialist platform that demanded political unity. In early fall the KPD appeared to be blocking progress and seeking singular advantages that countered the growing pressure for unity and genuine democracy. Political elections were scheduled for early 1946 in the U.S. Zone and would have to be held in the Soviet Zone soon after, when the weakness of KPD might be formally registered (elections in Austria and Hungary in November went strongly against the local Communist parties). Finally the SPD Central Committee was displaying increasing independence.

Sometime in September or early October the SMA and KPD leaders decided to reverse their position on unity. Launching a campaign for immediate unity might halt the popular trend toward the Socialists and improve the Communists' image as selfless promoters of workers' progress, thereby possibly forestalling election setbacks. Pieck and Ulbricht now publicly claimed that the time was ripe for unity and openly attacked the SPD leadership for allegedly harboring Nazis. By attempting to discredit the top Socialists, the KPD expected to strengthen its campaign for promoting unity from below.

They received a sharp jolt, however, from a speech by Otto Grotewohl on November 11, who was Chairman of the Berlin Central Committee, on the occasion of the SPD's independent celebration of the Russian Revolution. In analyzing the situation in Germany, he criticized the loss of territory east of the Oder-Neisse line (which Ulbricht had insisted was the penalty of German aggression as early as June 10), objected to dismantling of German industry, which had been conducted most ruthlessly by the SMA (and endorsed by both Ulbricht and Pieck during the summer), and challenged the Allied plans for controlled German industrial production (explicitly endorsed by the KPD). While the angle of the attack was obliquely aimed at the Allies in general, it also challenged parties that pledged unquestioned allegiance and provided no national alternative. In turning to zonal politics, Grotewohl again endorsed the concept of unity but for the first time reversed himself on the matter of timing. He rejected the arguments for urgency and immediacy and also questioned the desired method and scope of unity. Indeed, he introduced a new formula for unification that tended to mirror the now-discarded communist demands for the institutionalization of democratic reforms as the prerequisite for unity. He insisted that unity could not function unless it was the genuine desire of the members of both parties; this determination would require party referendums. No external pressure could be applied during this entire process of self-examination. Unity with the Communists must follow, not precede, the establishment of democratic and socialist reconstruction. Finally unity must be based on the creation of unified nationwide parties of the working class. In other words, the organization of national parties was intended to promote the establishment of democracy and socialism, to be followed by national reunification and then by self-determination of the respective parties on the issue of unity. This represented a major policy shift and was an attempt to seize the initiative from the KPD.

Ulbricht neatly reversed the order of Grotewohl's priorities: Unity of the working class must precede national reunification, and zonal unity of the working class should be the appropriate antecedent. Tactical lines were now clearly drawn between the Berlin Committee and the KPD.

By the end of January, pressure for unity from below created by purges of pro-Grotewohl elements and Soviet intervention had reached such dimensions that the SPD in the Soviet Zone was no longer organizationally viable. Unity on KPD terms now seemed only a matter of time. At that juncture, Grotewohl's only succor could have come from the Western Allied authorities, who were by then distrustful of a party that had initially been more Bolshevik than the KPD and now sought support through *embourgeoisement,* or from the Hannoverian SPD, which had gradually sharpened its criticism of the Berlin Central Committee.

The contents of the polemics and debates within the SPD are revealing both about the nature and scope of unity and the role the SPD could play in the grand design as perceived by the Berlin Central Committee, and about the proper function of the SPD in the Soviet Zone as viewed from the West. These original disputes among the Socialists became critical ideological and political schisms that had to be overcome before reconciliation between the two Germanys was conceivable by the SPD.

On the one side, Grotewohl maintained that the aim of the Soviets' German policy was to insure working-class domination of German political life as insurance of the indefinite preservation of a friendly attitude toward the USSR. Under such conditions, bolstered with adequate guarantees, Moscow would accept "parliamentary" democracy, which, of course, would not include anti-Soviet elements. Further, Grotewohl thought that he was the natural leader of a rejuvenated German socialism that would restore the solidarity of the left on a nationwide basis—a goal also sought by Moscow.

On the other side, Kurt Schumacher in Hannover held that the Soviet aims were to dominate Germany and central Europe through establishing standing "political armies" that would allow the Soviets gradually to reduce their direct intervention without jeopardizing their national interests. This aim would be achieved in their zone by the Communists' absorption and subordination of the Social Democrats. This view was clearly a reversion to the prewar socialist tradition of anti-Bolshevism that Grotewohl feared would merely nurture natural Soviet animosity against Socialists. Accordingly, he saw his dream of a consolidated German socialist movement imperiled unless he could counter the adverse Communist criticism by mollifying them on the issue of unity.

As the debate on the future of socialism in the East and party unity reached a climax in February 1946, Grotewohl and the other members of the Central Committee recognized the hard realities of their plight: They were isolated from their Western colleagues and estranged from their own rank and file. Grotewohl acknowledged that to unleash a struggle against the KPD would mean carrying on a fight against the occupation forces. Potsdam and the respective Four-Power accords had delegated the conduct of political life to each zonal commandant. The SPD could not accept such a fight. Moreover, continued resistance by the Central Committee would merely accelerate unity at the local level and further weaken the central authority of the SPD. Yet to dissolve the party unilaterally would mean abandoning loyal Socialists to possible communist victimization. Under such circumstances the Committee concluded that its best option for both immediate survival and the attainment of long-range goals of socialist leadership in Germany was to accept the KPD plan for unity and attempt to maximize socialist influence over the Communists from within the new party structure.[9]

On February 11, 1946, the Central Committee voted in favor of unification and the Socialist Unity party of Germany (SED) was established on April 22. Grotewohl was named cochairman of the SED and later Premier of the GDR, and the SPD in the Soviet Zone was effectively dismantled.

After witnessing the trauma of party unification, the Western SPD became divided about its future relations with SED. The majority interpreted the SED overt interference in the 1948 West Berlin municipal elections, its open support of the Soviet blockade, the subsequent purging of the former Socialists from the SED, and finally the suppression of the 1953 uprising as manifestations of communist "treachery" and subordination to Soviet priorities. A leftist minority, however, tended to excuse these actions as inevitable under the circumstances. This small group saw reconciliation with the SED as the only option for advancing the dual goals of promoting socialism in West Germany and securing greater freedom of maneuver for the SED against the Soviets in East Germany. This faction viewed the controversies of West German rearmament in 1953, NATO membership in 1954, and Soviet reunification bids in 1955 as lost opportunities when the Adenauer policy of "maintained tensions" should have been jettisoned in favor of greater acceptance of communist rule in East Germany. Events in Eastern Europe in 1956 and the Khrushchev 1958 ultimatum muted this opposition and the West German SPD enjoyed its greatest cohesion to date, siding with the government's policy of firmness against Soviet threats to the status quo, such as the Soviet ultimatum on Germany and Berlin made in November 1958.

Thus one important implication of the party unification and the subsequent communization of the Soviet Zone was that it demoralized and disoriented the SPD, forcing it onto the defensive against the Communists and the Christian Democrats. Each passing year seemed to confirm the correctness of the Adenauer policy, yet it was equally clear that Moscow had established increasingly rigid limits on the extent to which it would accept cooperation with the Adenauer government, concerning, for example, the release of war prisoners and establishment of diplomatic relations (which were gestures intended to influence the Geneva summit conference on the German problem). In these circumstances, the majority of the SPD leaders still nurtured the notion that ultimately only the Socialists would be regarded as sufficiently reliable by the Soviets to permit a genuine dialogue with the East German Communists;

yet it could countenance neither Soviet threats against the
status quo or East German obduracy.

It was in this general atmosphere that the 1959 Party Congress adopted the historic Bad Godesberg Program. It was
designed to preserve the party's socialist character but also to
establish a distinctly different form of Marxist ideology from
that of the SED, based on Christian ethics and Western philo-
sophical thought. The new program was intended to terminate
further factionalism and to rejuvenate the party by providing a
singularity of objectives that specified policy alternatives and
prospects for gaining political power. The Bad Godesberg Program was a crucial turning point in the rehabilitation of the SPD
within the West German polity. After a near-disastrous flirtation with communism, the program marked a new confidence
about the SPD role in FRG politics and its ability to deal with
the SED from a position of renewed strength. This cathartic
experience and the ensuing release from guilt over earlier complicity afforded the Socialists greater public acceptance as legitimate opponents of communism.

FROM COLLABORATION TO CONFRONTATION

Less than two weeks after the Soviets announced the sus-
pension of the Berlin blockade,[10] the German Parliamentary
Council, authorized by the Western Allies to formulate the
basis for a national government, adopted on May 8, 1949 the
Basic Law (Provisional Constitution) for the Federal Republic.
The Constitution of the German Democratic Republic was
adopted in March by a "People's Council" and approved by a
"German People's Congress" in May. The Presidium of the
People's Council announced on October 7 the creation of the
GDR.[11] On the same day West German Chancellor Konrad
Adenauer denounced the establishment of a separate German
state, since the legitimacy of the government had not been
authenticated by formally expressed public support. The creation of separate German states, both proclaiming independence
and sovereignty and the constitutional right to establish com-

mon institutions throughout Germany, was a definitive step
toward the partition of Germany and the creation of rival political entities.

In reaction to this de facto partitioning, the three Western
foreign ministers met in September 1950 in New York and
issued a communiqué calling for an end of the state of war,
authorization for the establishment of West German police
forces comparable to the GDR *Volkspolizei,* a revision of the
Occupation Statute, and an upward modification of the ceilings
on industrial production.[12] In October, the Cominform foreign
ministers met in Prague and concluded in response that a peace
treaty was the most desirable solution to the German problem
and that the initial step should be the creation of an all-German
Constituent Council, equally represented by East and West
Germany.[13]

In November Premier Grotewohl communicated with Adenauer and called for opening negotiations between the two
German states on the basis on the Prague Declaration.[14] In a
statement approved by the Bundestag, Adenauer declared that
the conditions for the formation of an all-German Constituent
Assembly was that delegates must be elected, not appointed.
Free elections required guaranteed personal freedom, political
liberty, and the prohibition of coercion (the disbandment of the
Volkspolizei). In a move in the opposite direction, the GDR
further consolidated its political viability, on January 27, 1951,
by signing an accord with Poland recognizing the Oder-Neisse
as a common border, a measure advocated by Walter Ulbricht
as early as June 1945. For the West it appeared that the Soviets
were deliberately offering unacceptable demands while permitting the GDR to establish systematically a separate German
political entity. The sincerity of the Soviet interests in reunification was now repeatedly challenged by both the Christian
Democrats and the Social Democrats in West Germany.

Between March and June 1951, the Four-Power foreign ministers held 74 meetings in Paris in a futile attempt to reconcile
differences over the German problem. The Soviet strategy was
to stress the urgency of a peace treaty and the establishment of
a "peace-loving" unified German state. Those who opposed

these objectives on whatever pretext, were then conveniently labeled revanchists, war-mongers, and imperialists.

In the winter of 1951 the FRG negotiated with the three Western powers contractual agreements terminating the Occupation Statute.[15] It also was genuinely involved with five other Western states in the formation of a European Defense Community, EDC (designed as a supranational community with common institutions, common armed forces, and a singular budget, but operating within the NATO framework). While these discussions were in progress, the USSR and GDR pursued two separate approaches. Moscow proposed in March the formation of a provisional all-German government as the necessary precursor for the establishment of a "unified, independent, democratic and peace-loving state." The other tack was to intensify polemics. GDR President Pieck declared in May that FRG integration with the West was a just cause for establishing the "armed defense of our country." Premier Grotewohl stated that the Western "contractual agreements" created a Korean-like situation and the danger of a fratricidal war of German against German. Vice Premier Ulbricht threatened Adenauer with "reprisals at the hands of the German people" and declared all members of the FRG Parliament as enemies of the people who would be suitably punished.[16]

The Western contractual agreements were signed by Bonn on May 26, and the GDR took immediate countermeasures. First, a security zone three miles wide was established along the entire East German border and the Baltic coast. All telephone communications between the Soviet Zone and West Berlin were cut, and freedom of travel was suspended; that is, all West Germans and West Berliners would have to apply for special visas to visit East Germany. (Travel from West to East Berlin was not impaired nor was Autobahn traffic between the FRG and Berlin.) These precipitous actions were justified by the National Committee of the East German Nationale Front (a "single unit" representing all political parties) because of Western "provocations" along the frontier. Indeed these provocations made it "unavoidably necessary" to establish a national East German army.[17]

In a series of diplomatic exchanges in 1952 and 1953, the Soviets amplified on their proposed all-German government. In order to insure that East German interests were not submerged by the more populous West Germany, equal representation was mandatory. The means for selecting representation, however, would remain at the discretion of each government. An all-German commission should be created immediately to resolve technical details and negotiate a final accord acceptable to both regimes, which in turn would jointly sponsor a provisional all-German government and then dissolve themselves. "The main task of the provisional all-German government should be the holding of free all-German elections," and the Four Powers should take steps to insure that such elections are held in "real freedom."[18]

For the Western powers the key factor in any reunification scheme must be free elections and complete endorsement of the principle of self-determination. With clear evidence of communist manipulation of the SPD and authoritarian control by the SED of the Nationale Front, the West rejected the Soviet proposal for creating a Four-Power electoral commission. Instead the West called for an impartial inspection of conditions for and supervision of the elections by a UN commission on Germany, which the Soviets blocked. Thus the two sides were deadlocked on the fundamental issue of elections.

During July 1953, Bonn advanced its own initiative, listing a number of conditions as prerequisites for fruitful discussions of reunification: (1) reopening of zonal frontiers, (2) destruction of the GDR's security zone, (3) restoration of freedom of travel, (4) freedom of the press, assembly, and political activity, and (5) guarantees of civil rights. Later, the Bonn government rejected a Soviet proposal made on August 15, charging that, like earlier Soviet propositions which were directed against NATO, this one was aimed at destroying the EDC and influencing the forthcoming West German election campaign that was concentrating mainly on the issue of German rearmament. Furthermore, the Soviet scheme would leave Germany with limited armed forces and no guarantee for either neutrality or security.

Finally, since Bonn did not recognize the East German regime as legitimate, it refused to have any contacts with the GDR.

After the elections, the Christian Democrats were sufficiently strong to force through a constitutional amendment in February 1954 necessary for participation in the EDC. The proposed organization was subsequently defeated by France. This action reinforced the move toward Bonn's accession to NATO, accepted in October 1954 and finally approved by the Bundestag in February 1955, over SPD opposition. In a related matter, during the abortive Four-Power Foreign Ministers Meeting in Berlin between January 25 and February 18, Molotov called for a European Collective Security Treaty. It was rejected because it would have necessitated dissolving NATO and the EDC, leaving the Soviet Union the dominant European power.

In denouncing the Soviet proposal and analyzing the failure of the Berlin conference, Adenauer stated that Moscow intended to maintain the status quo and ultimately to dominate all Europe. The German people would never accept partition, and the flow of refugees from the East should have indicated to Moscow that the Pieck-Grotewohl regime could not legitimately participate in any all-German functions or capacities. Molotov's notion of collective security was a compelling incentive to construct a genuine security system in Western Europe, which by its purely defensive nature would provide the USSR the security it requires. Any pan-European system must be based on equality and free consent, which would undermine Soviet control over Eastern Europe. Finally, he acknowledged that the German problem could not be solved in isolation from other cold-war issues, such as the Far East and disarmament. Bonn was prepared to participate in the general process for détente dealing with all contentious matters. But the highest priority for the Federal Government must be to ease the burden of the Germans in Berlin and the Soviet Zone.[19]

On May 5, 1955 Western occupation of the FRG was formally ended and Grotewohl used the occasion to define his government's terms for reunification; including annulment of the Paris Agreements admitting the FRG to NATO, immediate understanding between the two Germanys on the "removal of militarism" and on the preparation of free elections to an all-German National Assembly, a joint request for the withdrawal of all occupation troops and the conclusion of a peace treaty, and continuous consultations between the two Germanys on outstanding matters. Finally, the Austrian State Treaty on neutrality and reunification should be viewed as an appropriate antecedent for solving the German problem.[20] While this was an obvious attempt to block West German participation in Western security arrangements and to entice Bonn into a "centralist" position between East and West, there was no evidence that the GDR intended to impede its own integration into the Soviet bloc.

In March 1954 the Soviet government granted full recognition of the GDR as a sovereign state and in July appointed an ambassador. In August it annulled all decrees issued by Soviet military authorities, thus tacitly renouncing its political occupation status, but insisted that its troops would remain in the GDR under Four-Power agreements. (The Bundestag unanimously rejected the Soviets' right to create a German state, and the Western high commissioners announced that Moscow's action had not altered the situation and that their governments would continue to hold the USSR responsible for the Soviet Zone.) In response to the Paris Agreements, Moscow invited, in November 1954, the United States and 23 European states to a European security conference. Only East European countries attended—including the GDR. They agreed to the creation of a collective security system (the Warsaw Pact) signed in May 1955. Finally in January 1956 the GDR established its own national armed forces that were subsequently admitted to the Pact's Joint Military Command. The announcement was accompanied by a proposal from Grotewohl that the two Germanys pledge to refrain from the use of force against each other, support a European Collective Security Treaty, seek a common position on nuclear weapons, and normalize their relations.[21] Thus even before the explosive 20th Soviet Party

Congress in February 1956, the GDR was integrated into the political and security structures in Eastern Europe.

As this integrative process was developing, Moscow sought to improve on its relations with the West. In January 1955 Moscow announced that it had good relations with the GDR and was now prepared to normalize relations with Bonn, provided the Paris Agreements were not ratified, which would alter the security of Europe. On January 25, Moscow formally ended the state of war with Germany (the Western Allies did so in 1951). Bonn rejected the quid pro quo for its lack of participation in NATO and stated that ending the state of war would be a step toward normalization only if the Soviets agreed to self-determination in the Zone and the release of German prisoners as a first move. Bonn placed greater immediate emphasis on the issue of prisoner release than on reunification, and, in light of other Soviet global foreign policy initiatives, Moscow apparently perceived an increased need for greater accessibility and possibly influence in Bonn. In September Adenauer traveled to Moscow to gain release of nearly 10,000 prisoners and to establish diplomatic relations. At a press conference after the three-day summit meeting, Adenauer stated that normalizing relations with the USSR did not alter in any way Bonn's contention that it was the only legitimate government for all Germany or its treaty obligations with the West.

Thus 1955 witnessed modest changes in the German problem. Moscow had failed to stymie Bonn's entry into NATO but had insured GDR participation in its own pact. The Austrian State Treaty marked an improvement in the détente process. And the Four-Power summit conference during July in Geneva pledged that "reunification of Germany by means of free elections shall be carried out in conformity with the national interests and European security." Such vague wording subsequently permitted the Soviet Union to place regional defense requirements above German national interests on the issue of election supervision. Finally, the establishment of relations between the FRG and the Soviet Union was viewed in both countries as means for asserting their respective interests and influence in the others' capital. However peripheral, some movement had been registered.

Conventional wisdom now holds that the reason for Khrush-chev's modest *demarche* with Bonn and attempted reconcilia-tion with Tito was his concern about a major break with China, increasingly apparent since 1954. To present Peking with a solid socialist opposition would require accommodation of the Tito heresy, consolidation and legitimization of the GDR, and a minimalization of the West German challenge to East Euro-pean stability. All three aims might require Soviet acceptance of some manifestations of national communism. If successful, Khrushchev could then deal with China with a reduced threat of a two-front confrontation. Acceptance of separate roads to socialism, however, necessitated destalinization and the over-hauling of the tenets of Soviet rule. Khrushchev effectively exposed Stalin's criminality but failed to provide alternative guidelines for East European leaders, resulting in social uncer-tainty and political vacuums.

With the continuing Soviet pressure on the German problem and repeated distraction of Allied attention with other interna-tional crises in the late 1940s and early 1950s, the Adenauer government refused to relinquish German territorial claims in Eastern Europe or its role as the sole representative of German interests in international affairs. To reinforce its claims for sole German responsibilities, it devised, in December 1955, the Hallstein Doctrine, whereby Bonn pledged to sever diplo-matic ties with any state recognizing the GDR.[22] The policy was intended to isolate the GDR and demonstrate to the So-viets that their position east of the Elbe River held inherent liabilities that could be converted to political assets under more normal conditions.

Adenauer's concept of "maintained tensions" presupposed that relaxing tensions necessitated some quid pro quo from the Eastern side. Until matching moves toward détente were made, Bonn was determined to continue pressure for a modifi-cation of the intransigent Soviet stand against reunification based on self-determination and free elections. Normalization of relations between the two Germanys was to incorporate reciprocal moves towards the establishment of common institutions and social goals. Mutual incompatability of political aims, however, led to doctrinal rigidity of the two sides, reinforced by their respective strengths or weaknesses in any bargaining process.

While Bonn focused on the problem of reunification, East Germany was obsessed with the issue of legitimization. The GDR was the first Leninist experiment in such an industrialized and Western-oriented society and a potentially dangerous threat to Soviet influence in Europe, as demonstrated by the 1953 uprising. The continuing instability through 1955 probably forced the Soviet decision to accept the risks to Moscow's Western relations associated with the creation of a "rump" communist German state.

The issue was not whether to create a separate German communist state, but how much sovereignty to grant it and when to do so. Stalin told Milovan Djilas in April 1945 that the Soviets intended from the outset to establish a socialist state within their zone.[23] Also, the open question of reunification, peace, and the viability of zonal administrations held clear assurances that the USSR could preserve its Four-Power responsibilities for participating in German affairs. The formation and rearmament of the FRG, the uprisings in 1953 and 1956, and finally the domestic crises with the GDR between 1958 and 1961, however, forced Moscow to extend greater sovereignty to East Berlin in an effort to enhance its stability. Yet, in neither the 1972 Berlin Protocols nor the 1964 or the 1975 Soviet-East German Friendship Treaty were Soviet rights unequivocally renounced. This ambiguity produced imprecise Western perceptions of Soviet intentions regarding the German problem. To enhance GDR legitimacy, Moscow repeatedly cast its moves as an action-reaction syndrome triggered by Western provocations. Such maneuvers clouded Western conclusions of when the Soviets finally endorsed the concept of two separate and sovereign Germanys, and subsequently how to use the partition to advantage in the West. These were the central issues of the German problem in the period between 1957 and 1964.

STRUCTURAL CHANGES IN THE EAST

After the political turmoil in Eastern Europe during 1956 and the consolidation of Khrushchev's leadership by purging the Politburo in February 1957, Moscow returned to a more assertive policy toward Bonn. Bulganin addressed a personal letter to Adenauer expressing dissatisfaction with West German foreign affairs since the establishment of diplomatic relations. In April, Moscow sent a more strongly worded note denouncing NATO bases in West Germany and the provision of tactical nuclear weapons for Bonn's use. The Federal Republic responded in May to this "grotesque and unparalleled interference in West German affairs" by asserting that it had a legitimate right to insure its security with nuclear weapons as long as the USSR continued to block international accord on disarmament. An earlier West German note agreed to open talks on a consular agreement but rejected the revised Soviet formula for reunification: a solution to be achieved through direct negotiations between the two Germanys. Bonn insisted as a quid pro quo that Moscow release all German *civilian* political prisoners as agreed in the 1955 talks (the POWs had already been freed). A deadlock resulted and was broken only with agreement on a modest trade and consular accord in April 1958 and the release of civilian detainees.

Khrushchev tried to capitalize on the Soviet Sputnik success by introducing in October 1957 the Rapacki Plan for a "nuclear free zone" in central Europe. The scheme was intended to deny the West Germans nuclear weapons and to demonstrate Soviet restraint at a time when it seemingly enjoyed a strategic advantage. But such dramatic disarmament proposals failed to mask the rapidly growing public uncertainty in East Germany.

Soviet diplomatic communication throughout 1958 repeatedly endorsed the East German contention that the German problem should be resolved by negotiations between the two Germanys, not through free elections. This reversal from the position held in 1955 denied the East German public of the last hope for modification of the Grotewohl regime. Popular morale sagged to new lows and defections to the West substantially increased.

On November 10, 1958, Khrushchev announced his demands for creation of a Free City of West Berlin under the
concept of three independent political entities. West Berlin's
status was to be guaranteed by the Four Powers and perhaps
the UN. Under the agreement, East Germany would guarantee
access to the Free City, in return for the termination of all
subversive activities in West Berlin. Finally, if the Western
Allies would not accept the Soviet demands within six months,
Moscow would sign a bilateral treaty with the GDR, delegating
all access rights to the Free City to East Berlin.[24]

Khrushchev's ultimatum was the most risky course of action
on the German question the Kremlin had taken since the Stalin
era. It indicated that the existing leadership had consolidated
its political position after the inadequately prepared flirtation
with the concept of national communism. Moscow had vigorously reasserted its priorities in Germany; that is, it insured the
viability of the communist regime in the Soviet Zone. In one
sense, the new initiative served to deflect Soviet domestic critics who had been demanding greater liberalization and a higher
quality of life, as well as to appease the conservative opposition
who were apprehensive about earlier trends toward accommodation with the West. In another vein, it replayed a persistent
refrain in the Sino-Soviet dispute: consolidation in Europe before squarely facing China.

The Western Allies and the FRG were surprised by the
Khrushchev ultimatum. They refused to be coerced into negotiations under duress, but they did agree to open discussions on
the Soviet proposal. Moscow then suspended its timetable, but
insisted that it would not negotiate on the German problem
without the presence of the East Germans.[25] The Soviets accepted a minimum objective of convening a Four-Power foreign ministers' meeting in Geneva, between May 11, and June
20, 1959, with both East and West German observers. The
positions of both sides were restated in terms that revealed
even deeper splits, such as the West's demands for the reunification of Berlin after free elections. Another session, in July
and August, led to a complete stalemate, but also to the suspen-
sion of Soviet pressure on Berlin. Khrushchev had achieved an
important intermediary prize: an invitation for the first state

visit to the United States for a Soviet head of state, a critical move in his struggle with China and campaign to enhance Soviet global prestige.[26]

Germany did not figure prominently in East-West relations for the next two years; the Kremlin was sufficiently distracted by other priorities that it did not respond in a consistent manner to the deteriorating domestic situation in the GDR (although it had been on the agenda for the abortive May 1960 Paris summit conference attended by the United States and the Soviet Union). Germany was, however, a major subject at the summit meeting in June 1961 between Khrushchev and Kennedy in Vienna. Khrushchev presented the new president two memoranda demanding, *inter alia,* that the question be settled, again within six months, on the basis of the three German entities. Kennedy departed with the statement "It will be a cold winter," indicating division among his advisers about the urgency of the threat of unilateral Soviet action and the importance of a coordinated Western response. Khrushchev again surprised the West by publishing the two memoranda on June 10 and, then, five days later, conducting a nationwide television address. The strategic balance had now changed, he claimed, in the Soviets' favor, adding a new dimension to Moscow's demands.[27]

On the same day, SED party Chairman Walter Ulbricht held a rare press conference, which was noteworthy for its variance with the Soviet position. He ruled out unequivocally the sealing off of West Berlin. "Nobody intends to put up a Wall."[28] More critical, West Berlin, he claimed, lies within the GDR and is part of its territory. While arguing that access rights and the conclusion of a peace treaty required direct negotiations between the FRG and GDR, he paralleled the Soviet position, but in insisting that West Berlin was on East German territory, he raised a fundamental and long-lasting controversy with the Soviet Union.

First, the Soviets could not argue that West Berlin should be a free city if the bases for its independence were challenged by rival East German claims of sovereignty. Second, if the Soviets accepted the East German position, it would represent a de facto extension of a measure of sovereignty and independent decision-making to the GDR that Moscow would not accept. Finally, endorsement of the GDR assertions would minimize the relevancy of Four-Power guarantees of the status of the Free City and maximize the importance of East Germany's authority over access rights. All three prospects threatened to undermine Soviet status in Germany under Four-Power agreements and reduce its influence in German affairs, which the proposed structural changes were intended to enhance. Although Khrushchev did adopt temporarily the East German phraseology during the height of the crisis, these dilemmas continued to plague the bargaining position of the Soviet Union and East Germany until roughly 1972.

There were policy dilemmas for the West as well. Kennedy had a close personal rapport with British Prime Minister Macmillan and a deep admiration for General de Gaulle. But there was a marked incompatibility between the new Kennedy administration and the hardened West German Chancellor and his "testy" Ambassador to Washington, Wilhelm Grewe. There was a growing feeling in the new administration that Adenauer's policy of dealing from a position of strength had been largely unsuccessful in demonstrating that the GDR was not viable. Confronted now with a seemingly determined Soviet stance, West German intransigence could prove awkward and counterproductive. Consequently, when the United States began searching for policy options after Khrushchev's surprise move over Berlin, it frequently omitted consultations with Bonn, which proved to be a serious oversight.

Kennedy's general approach to the crisis was to strengthen the NATO Alliance and establish a coordinated Western position. Former Secretary of State Dean Acheson was appointed head of a special task force to study policy alternatives. The panel concluded that Berlin was not a problem but a pretext. Soviet intentions were not to solve the German problem, but to test the political will and determination of the United States. Khrushchev had precipitated the crisis because his fear of nuclear war had diminished. The West's position should be to convince Moscow that it is prepared to accept nuclear war rather than a change in the status quo. This should be done by a prompt strengthening of the conventional and nuclear forces of the United States. If Moscow signed a bilateral treaty and the GDR then interrupted access, the United States should counter with an airlift. If unsuccessful, a ground probe of Allied forces too strong to be stopped by East German troops alone— a corps of two divisions—should then be launched. The objective would not be the tactical defeat of Pact forces, but to demonstrate the resolve of the Allies to escalate to nuclear war if necessary. The panel concluded that the military preparations might deter Khrushchev, but nonetheless the West should consider a plausible negotiating strategy, focusing on strengthening the West's position in Berlin.[29]

The report was criticized by the administration's Soviet experts, who stressed that increased military readiness, rather than an anticipated showdown, and a specific negotiating strategy would best defuse the crisis. The President chose a combination of both: a rapid buildup of conventional forces by the United States on the Continent, sufficient to convince Khrushchev that vital American interests were involved that would preclude any easy seizure of the city. He called for the other Western Allies to increase their forces as well and to consider a concerted negotiating position.

Khrushchev responded by announcing a buildup of Soviet forces and an increase in the defense budget, but explicitly ruled out the possibility of a new Berlin blockade as a means of pressuring the West.[30] East Germany, however, officially announced that as of August 1 it would require all foreign aircraft to register with a GDR flight center, rather than with the Allied Safety Control Center. The decree was immediately rejected by the West. It may have been a coordinated tactic, but it now appears to have been a deliberate unilateral assertion of East German interests. It was never even verbally endorsed by Moscow. (At the time Western analysts interpreted the East German ploy as an orchestrated increase in tensions, soon amplified by Khrushchev's threat of nuclear annihilation over Berlin, rather than indications of diverging aims.)

On July 8, Khrushchev revealed that an underlying objective

in the crisis was to gain Western recognition that "the Socialist countries are not inferior to the forces of the Western powers." Given equal forces, there must be equal rights and equal opportunities.[31] He did not indicate what opportunities he was seeking or how they would be used; nor did he cite the need for equal restraints.

On July 25, Kennedy made a key move in the developing crisis when he discussed the position of the United States in a nationwide address. He called for an increase of $3.5 billion for military spending, in addition to the $3 billion requested in the spring. The new money was to be allocated exclusively for strengthening conventional forces. "There is peace in Berlin today," he said. "The source of world trouble and tension is Moscow, not Berlin. And if war begins, it will have begun in Moscow not Berlin."[32] But, he continued, we do not want military considerations to dominate the thinking of either East or West and suggested conducting quiet exploratory talks in formal or informal meetings.

The reasons for the exclusive emphasis on improved conventional military readiness were twofold. Washington was confronted with the classical problem of determining what preparations would be clearly perceived as precautionary, not provocative. The posture of the United States, therefore, was to be strengthened in a manner that would not be directly threatening to Moscow, but that also would underscore the determination of the United States to counter the Soviet proposal. At the same time, the United States was seeking an alternative strategy between "holocaust or humiliation." The Berlin buildup was the initial step in the development of the multiple-optional doctrine of flexible response.[33]

There were rumors throughout the West at that time that the Soviets would have to "wall in" the East Germans. In the first six months of 1961, over 100,000 East Germans fled to the West, and after Khrushchev's speech on July 8, panic caused 8231 to flee by mid-July. The total number of refugees over 15 years was three million, but the figures were rapidly increasing. Yet Western authorities did not anticipate a partition of the sectors.[34]

This miscalculation was due to three erroneous assumptions: (1) the Soviets would not take any physical actions until a bilateral peace treaty was signed with the GDR, thereby legalizing any provocative moves; (2) the Soviets would hardly jeopardize their position in Berlin under the Four-Power agreements and, therefore, any partitioning would be between the Soviet Sector and the GDR, where the West had little authority; and (3) the major threat, therefore, was interference by the Soviet Union and East Germany with Western rights in West Berlin, which should be the focal point of concerted Western action.

But the Allies were split on the issue of forming an orchestrated policy. Britain was in a serious financial crisis, its strategic reserves were deployed to Kuwait, and the Cabinet was debating a proposal to reduce the size of its forces in Germany. Under these conditions the British government strongly endorsed the reasonableness of Kennedy's willingness to negotiate and avoided any public commitment to strengthen its military posture.

French strategic reserves were also deployed overseas at that time in Tunisia in the dispute over Bizerte. Therefore, Paris could not shift significant forces to Germany without mobilizing reserves. Even more important, de Gaulle adamantly refused to consider negotiations in light of Khrushchev's exorbitant demands. He concluded that it would be disastrous for the West to negotiate under duress.

The Federal Republic had the most to lose in either a military confrontation or a negotiated settlement and strongly endorsed the French position. Bonn's "no-negotiation" stand was based on the danger that any bargaining with the East would require some contact with the GDR and, therefore, afford it some degree of de facto recognition. But the "no-negotiation" policy led to Bonn's increasing isolation as the tempo of the crisis quickened.

The communiqué issued by the NATO Council on August 8 ignored both a request by the United States for extensive troop strengthening and the negotiation issue but called for reunification on the basis of self-determination. Yet, after departing the

Council meeting, Secretary Rusk indicated the most plausible Western course of action: "I think there will be negotiations. It is only a question of how and where that remains to be worked out."[35] (There is no firm evidence indicating whether this statement revealed the actual state of confidential diplomatic exchanges between the United States and the Soviet Union on the issue or whether it was merely an assumption the United States had made based on earlier precedents. It was probably the latter.)

The Political Consultative Committee of the Warsaw Pact met in Moscow on August 3 to endorse the intermediary position of the Soviet Union and East Germany in the crisis, both unilateral actions and negotiations. Moscow had intensified the rhetorical pitch of its polemics in an attempt, it now appears, to deter Western military response when it opted for intermediate gains.[36] But the accelerated bombast terrorized the East German populace more than the West and prompt action was necessary to block the flood of refugees. Accordingly, the PCC adopted a joint declaration, issued on August 12, appealing to the GDR to take all measures necessary against the threats to its security presented by militaristic and revanchist policies of the FRG and West Berlin, including the establishment of effective border controls.[37]

The GDR Council of Ministers acted on this declaration and issued its own decree, establishing forms of controls "customary on the frontiers of every sovereign state," including those between the Western sectors and East Berlin, the capital of the GDR.[38] The Soviets had jettisoned their maximum demands and even foregone the minimal aim of negotiations and accepted the goal of modest structural modification of the status quo. At midnight on August 13 the border between the sectors was sealed.

The scope of the West's surprise can only partially be measured by the tardiness and ineffectiveness of its responses. The initial reaction by the United States was made on August 13 when a statement was issued through the State Department citing East German actions as violations of existing Four-Power agreements that would be protested through appropriate channels. Three days later, Adenauer told Soviet Ambassador Smirnov that Bonn would not initiate any actions that might endanger good relations with Moscow.[39] (West Germany then was in the midst of a national election campaign in which Adenauer's political latitude was constrained by the vigorous reactions of his leading contender, SPD leader Willy Brandt.)

As mayor of West Berlin, Brandt made the strongest objections. On August 16, he sent a personal letter to Kennedy, calling the Wall the most serious development for the city since the 1948 blockade and requested that the security of the Western sectors be reinforced by a formal proclamation of a new three-power status for West Berlin.

On the seventeenth, the three powers delivered a formal protest denouncing the Soviet action as a flagrant violation of existing agreements and Britain and France announced the reinforcement of their forces in Germany. The United States sent Vice President Johnson and retired General Clay with Kennedy's personal reply to Brandt, and also dispatched a small 1500-man battle group into its sector. Eventually, sizeable American reserves forces were deployed to Germany and maintained there until 1963. The objective of these token Western reactions was to inspire hope and confidence among the demoralized West Berliners; it was not to demolish the Wall. The failure of the West to prevent the division of Berlin concentrated increasing Western attention on the viability of West Berlin and on the credibility of the three powers' rights in the City.[40]

The Wall was another turning point in the postwar German problem. The Soviet action had successfully altered both the structure and the psychology of the status quo. The division of the two Germanys was now completed at a relatively low cost in cold-war terms. It lowered the temperature of the cold war and probably contributed to the decision by the United States to accelerate its intervention in Southeast Asia, especially Laos, and to the expansion of its strategic forces. There was a more obvious linkage between the Wall and the reactions of the United States during the Cuban Missile Crisis. Yet it gave the

Soviet Union the respite it needed in Europe for the next and most dangerous phase of the Sino-Soviet dispute.

While Germany was the focal point of the Berlin crisis, the GDR played the key role of demanding the final division as critical for its viability and legitimization. The FRG, for its part, was the least significant actor. When the West could not agree on concerted policy, the important interactions reverted to bilateral exchanges between the superpowers. It is interesting to note that without direct "hot-line" links, the limits of conventional diplomatic communications forced both Kennedy and Khrushchev to use the vehicles of public addresses and extensive press conferences to signal their intentions.

Speaking to an adversary through the public media was confusing on two separate issues: the need for confidential exchanges indispensable for diplomatic accommodation and the necessity for generating national charisma critical for crystallizing public consensus behind important foreign policy moves. The resulting overlapping led to misperceptions and ambiguities, experienced again in the Cuban Missile Crisis, and subsequently, to the establishment of direct, high-speed, confidential communications.

The central factor in American misperceptions, however, was the estimation that the Soviets had no intermediate position between unilateral action and negotiations, as they had demonstrated in 1959. But precisely because the earlier strategy had failed to produce the desired results should have suggested that it could not be reemployed under even more demanding circumstances. This underestimation may have stemmed from the simplistic views of Soviet cold-war diplomacy widely held at the time, whereby confrontations were largely confined to single issues with ongoing problems, such as disarmament, being linked only tangentially to the immediate crisis. While this was an accurate description, it fostered Western expectations of black-and-white solutions to crises that ignored the possibility of Soviet diplomatic innovations.[41] When Soviet adventuristic foreign policy became slightly moderated and American threat preceptions remained rela-

tively consistent between 1962 and 1965, initiatives for penetrating the stalemated cold-war doctrinaire positions originated
with lesser forces, France and the post-Godesberg SPD. The
West German opposition gradually became the prime mover in
seeking a fundamental modification of the new rigidity imposed on central Europe by the Wall.

Chapter II

Precursors to Negotiations

THE EVALUATION OF WEST GERMAN DOMESTIC POLITICS AND FOREIGN POLICIES

The physical partitioning of Berlin and the final division of Germany underscored the conclusion that for a variety of reasons the Adenauer government's stand on reunification was becoming increasingly ineffective. First, the GDR had not been isolated within Eastern Europe; its position had been measurably strengthened and consummated by the Soviet-East German Friendship Treaty of 1964. Then, after it had been insulated from the West, it generated an economic miracle second only to that of the FRG and demonstrated that its system was viable, despite continued individual dissatisfaction and defections. On the international scale, its viability had become a function either of world diplomatic recognition, increasingly difficult for Bonn to block, or of military strength and Warsaw Pact consensus, an option detrimental to West German interests. However, the GDR remained a pawn in East-West relations, even though it now had gained a degree of diplomatic initiative in the negative sense of demonstrating the inapplicability of Bonn's decade-old policy of reunification. Finally, NATO solidarity with Bonn and the sharp increase in military preparedness during the crisis paradoxically were manifestations of the West's defensive attitude and its reluctance to use force to ameliorate the partition or resolve the German problem. Membership in the Western community could not be employed to generate a military posture that could advance Bonn's interests in reunification.[42]

[29]

The public shock expressed by West Germany over the implications of the construction of the Wall and NATO's inability to rectify this dramatic alteration in the status quo was coupled with the growing disenchantment about the overall relevance of international developments to East-West German problems, such as the slowdown in Western integration that was gradually eroding the leverage Bonn hoped to apply against the GDR and the USSR, the Soviet-American confrontations in the Congo and Cuba, which had demonstrated the precise limitations of Moscow's capability to support overseas military contingencies and had promoted the USSR to strengthen its posture in central Europe as an immediate alternative, the Sino-Soviet dispute, which had now reached unprecedented dimensions in the history of communism, and imparted uncertainties about Soviet behavior in Eastern Europe, and the fact that both Washington and Paris were showing increasing interest in promoting rapprochement with Moscow which might compete with Bonn's interests if they remained irreconcilable. Thus, in the interval between 1961 and 1964 (roughly from the Berlin crisis through the Friendship Treaty), traditional West German fears of isolation and estrangement began to emerge that nurtured independent thoughts among a growing number of intellectuals, journalists, and policy makers.

Professor Karl Jaspers was one of the first prominent figures to criticize publicly the entire structure of Bonn's reunification policy. He called for the abandonment of the policy to reunify Germany through establishment of common institutions and the concentration of government efforts instead of trying to improve the welfare of the people within the GDR.[43] This clarion call intensified public debate on the issue and initially forced all four major West German political parties to retrench and conduct general policy reappraisals.[44] As late as 1965, Gerhard Schröder, foreign minister in the CDU/FDP coalition, reaffirmed that "no government, constitutionally sworn as it is to act on behalf of all Germans and to restore German unity, could abandon the policy of reunification. . . . To do so would help to consolidate the unnatural and unjust partition of our country without bringing peace and security to Europe; and would perpetuate a dangerous source of tension in central Europe indefinitely. . . . Our policy must be not to arouse false hopes, but to establish relations between East and West based on mutual trust and thus enable us to remove first of all, the minor sources of tension, but subsequently the major ones as well."[45]

But when the FDP joined the coalition government in October 1963 and, more significantly, when Adenauer relinquished the chancellorship to Ludwig Erhard, the father of West German economic recovery, a modest erosion occurred in the policy of "maintained tensions." Contacts were broadened at the semiofficial level. Cultural exchanges were increased and permanent West German trade missions were established in all East European capitals, except Prague. In October 1965 the Evangelical Church of Germany published a formal declaration calling for the renunciation of German territorial claims in Poland and official recognition of the Oder-Neisse border. In the summer of 1966, the SPD reopened direct contacts with the SED and proposed that the two parties exchange speakers for their respective rallies and congresses. The SED accepted the offer but then reversed itself, having gained a token of recognition in the process. Both parties then used the news media to address specific questions to each other. Finally, the SPD sent to the SED Party Congress, held in April 1967, detailed proposals for expanding both interparty and inner-German relations and for easing the burdens of divided Germany step by step.

The contacts between the SPD and SED were by far the most important of these early exchanges. They indicated that the changes incorporated in the Bad Godesberg formula were creating genuine soul-searching within the party rank and file during the period after the Wall was built and that psychological adjustments were being made (see below). There was also tangible evidence that a growing majority of the membership was prepared to break with the traditional SPD policy of penetrating and then undermining the SED from within. Indeed, these contacts represented tacit SPD recognition of the SED's political viability, but not its legitimacy.

In March 1966 the Erhard government made the first open breach with the former positions by announcing a new "opening to the East."[46] In a diplomatic note delivered to 115 states, including those in Eastern Europe (except the GDR with which Bonn did not have diplomatic relations), it proposed negotiations on an accord for the reduction of nuclear weapons in Europe and a prohibition on the transfer of warheads to non-nuclear nations, a major concern of the Warsaw Pact countries in the light of Bonn's possible participation in the NATO's nuclear Multilateral Force. It also suggested that the Pact nations, including the GDR, conclude an agreement with the FRG banning the use of force in settling international disputes. The East Europeans responded that there were so many caveats attached to the proposal that it was both cynical and unacceptable. For example, the reduction of nuclear weapons was accompanied by a demand that the nuclear powers halt further production of all nuclear warheads—an unlikely prospect. The note also insisted that Germany continued in international law to exist as the political entity within the December 1937 boundaries until a freely elected all-German government should formally recognize other frontiers. This disqualified the note's proposal to open negotiations with Poland on Bonn's territorial claims. Likewise the FRG's insistence that it was the sole representative of the interests of the expelled Sudeten Germans negated Czechoslovak hopes that the 1938 Munich Agreement would be renounced by the FRG. Finally, prospects for improving relations with the GDR were reduced by Bonn's refusal to accept the existence of another German political entity. Thus, the new opening could not generate favorable responses; it was condemned as a veiled attempt to gain concessions by appearing conciliatory but devoid of adequate incentives or modifications in earlier positions. It remained a clear effort to isolate the GDR.

Roger Morgan has correctly observed that the pace of change in Bonn's policy toward both Eastern Europe and the GDR was governed at that time by the right wing of the CDU and the threat of defections to the National Democratic party (NDP), not by the opposition, which had already initiated independent contributions for a new approach.[47] But these moves were still too embryonic and the GDR too unresponsive; thus they failed to arouse sufficient public attention to become an issue during the 1965 national elections, when the CDU/CSU retained its plurality with 47.6 percent, the SPD fell to 39.3 percent, and the FDP polled 9.5 percent of the electorate.

The election results and the criticism by its own left wing about the ineffectiveness of earlier gestures toward the East prompted the SPD to introduce major revisions of its party platform during the June 1966 Party Conference. The SPD deputy parliamentary leader at the time, Helmut Schmidt, told the conference that the CDU policy of "strength" had failed unequivocally.[48] After lively debate, the conference adopted a resolution calling for the Federal Republic to play a more positive role in all aspects of the German problem, a definitive shift of emphasis from reunification to the welfare of East Germans, a reversal of the Hallstein Doctrine in Eastern Europe, and provisions for greater security for the East Europeans such as abrogating the Munich Agreement, and adopting a compromise formula on the Oder-Neisse border. Finally, it advocated the pursuit of a policy of peaceful coexistence with the GDR and broader contacts at all levels.[49] This new platform was the basis for the exchange of communications with the SED in 1966 and 1967 and the premise for SPD participation in the Grand Coalition.

The impact of the change in the SPD's Eastern policy had a discernable influence on the evolution of West German domestic politics. In December 1966 the Erhard administration fell, largely over domestic economic problems, but the SPD's terms for entering a coalition of the two major parties dealt primarily with foreign policy issues, including the promotion of international détente, acceptance of the nuclear nonproliferation treaty, modification of the Hallstein Doctrine to permit diplomatic relations with communist countries, and adoption of a more flexible policy toward East Germany, without extending it formal recognition. These terms were only partially endorsed in Chancellor Georg Kiesinger's maiden speech before the Bundestag, in which he dropped the label "Soviet Occupied

Zone" for the GDR and enumerated 15 specific areas for intensifying contact with East Germany. He omitted demands for reunification but refused to recognize the GDR and did not modify sufficiently the FRG's position on other issues to provide the basis for East European endorsement.[50]

The new government's proposals for widening relations with the GDR included freedom of travel, broader trade and credits, establishment of joint economic projects, wider cultural exchanges, and the appointment of commissioners to discuss means for improving the welfare of East Germans, that is, the practical application of the SPD's policy of accommodation through small steps. Inherent in these proposals was the fact that they extended a measured de facto recognition of the GDR regime. That is, Bonn was prepared to accept East Berlin as the capital of the GDR and the government as responsible for its public administration. This trend toward de facto, not legal recognition, was enhanced when the chancellor endorsed in April 1967 the SPD messages to the SED and addressed a series of declaratory statements and notes directly to Premier Willi Stoph citing specific proposals for expanding contacts between East and West Germany. In the March 1968 Annual State of the Nation Address, Kiesinger offered to negotiate on German problems directly with Stoph, if sufficient progress could be made in preliminary discussions to assure satisfactory results.[51]

But the SPD added further weight to its policy of adjustment at the 1968 party conference when it called for the FRG to "respect and recognize" the existing frontiers in Eastern Europe (implying those also of the GDR), pending the conclusion of a final peace treaty ending World War II. Before the April 1969 party conference, two provincial party organizations passed resolutions calling for full recognition of the GDR and Party Chairman Willy Brandt publicly pledged that the SPD would cooperate fully with East Berlin at all levels below formal recognition under international law. At the crucial 1969 conference, the SPD adopted, by 344 to 10 votes, a platform for the forthcoming national elections that accepted the recognition of the "statelike existence" of East Germany—a key issue that contributed to the SPD/FDP election victory that year.

Thus in the six years between the Berlin and Czechoslovak crises, important changes had emerged in domestic politics that had a corresponding impact on Bonn's inner-German politics or *Deutschlandpolitik*. The CDU/FDP had made minor moves toward the East European nations while perpetuating the policy of isolating the GDR. The SPD, however, had undergone the more cathartic experience of a decade-long period of ideological rejuvenation. By the late 1960s, the SPD, not the CDU, was psychologically conditioned to make the concessions to Eastern Europe and the GDR necessary to participate in the détente process. That is, only the SPD was prepared to accept existing boundaries and grant East Berlin a degree of recognition.

The importance of the Grand Coalition's policy was that it abandoned the concept of "maintained tensions," without requiring either a quid pro quo or sacrificing basic aims. Normalization of relations could be advanced by means of taking a series of confidence-building small steps as intermediate moves toward the final solution of the German problem. In reality, this gave the FRG the diplomatic initiative, and forced the GDR, Poland, and Czechoslovakia into the embarrassing "reversed" position of compelling them to pursue their own policies of "maintained tensions" toward Bonn that inevitably had wide-ranging implications for all East European states.

The advantages Bonn gained from the new opening were inaccurately perceived at the time. Former governments had concluded that the greatest leverage against the GDR could be accrued by incorporating inner-German policies with those relating to all Eastern Europe. Any reconciliation with Eastern Europe was designed partly to demonstrate the intransigence of the GDR and thereby promote its isolation within the Warsaw Pact. But this strategy tended to strengthen the bonds between the respective East European diplomatic positions: the issues of borders, territorial claims and responsibilities for those expelled were linked firmly with East Berlin's demands for international recognition, thus aligning the East Europeans in tandem behind the GDR. For the East Europeans, West German recognition of their borders was an absolutely essential prerequisite for their national security and normalization of relations, that is, the precondition for détente. Thus, Bonn's demands for reunification perpetuated the East Europeans' stake in keeping Germany divided.[52] Accommodation of FRG interest in solving the German problem could only follow genuine détente and acceptance of the GDR.

Rumania was the first Pact nation to conclude that this posture presented both the threat of expanding Soviet hegemony and an opportunity for developing an independent foreign policy initiative that might establish new norms for relations and behavior between members of the Pact.

RUMANIA'S DIPLOMATIC INITIATIVE

Political legitimacy, stability, and security have been the key priorities for the communist parties of Eastern Europe and the Soviet Union since the end of World War II. Yet, after a quarter century of communist rule in Czechoslovakia, the 1968 crisis proved the most dangerous threat ever to Soviet interests in Eastern Europe. Earlier uprisings had challenged directly Soviet security, but the Dubcek Action Program sought the most far-reaching reforms yet of the Soviet model for socialist progress and therefore potentially undermined the legitimacy of the entire Soviet system. Rumania played the central role during this period in reinterpreting socialist understanding of the German question, in probing Soviet tolerance for deviating from accepted policy, and in moderating East German intransigence on its terms for legitimacy and security.

When internal stability and legitimacy became key concerns after the 1953 uprising, the GDR quickly emerged as the chief proponent of bloc unity and integration. Soviet military presence was viewed as a symbol of Moscow's support for GDR independence, and Pact solidarity was seen as a demonstration of its international recognition. The urgency East Berlin attached to the cohesion of the socialist commonwealth inevitably placed it at variance with Bucharest. Since the withdrawal of Soviet troops in 1958, Rumania has held the opposite view of the political value of Soviet military presence and has perceived many aspects of bloc integration as vehicles for the extension of Soviet authority. Rumania tended to capitalize on the same issues the GDR expected would accelerate integration to establish its own autonomy within the bloc. That is, they used the same issues for the opposite objectives.

The first such problem that became apparent to the West was Khrushchev's attempt to overcome the growing economic malaise, which was becoming evident as early as 1960 in the USSR and Eastern Europe. He introduced his own notions for mobilizing the existing commercial organization of the bloc, the Council of Mutual Economic Assistance (CEMA), into a more efficient mechanism. He sought to incorporate supernational planning mechanisms that would allocate resources and markets according to a prescribed division of labor following lines of existing comparative economic advantages. This scheme would have intensified investment and production in finished industrial products in the GDR and Czechoslovakia and compelled Rumania and Bulgaria to sustain continued emphasis on expanding agricultural production rather than on industrialization. Rumania strongly objected, using Leninist arguments to justify the most rapid conversion possible to an industrialized economy. Its refusal in 1962 and 1963 to participate in the grand design for accelerating integration and the economic efficiency of the bloc polarized Eastern Europe within its own "mini cold war" between the GDR and Rumania.[53] Rumanian "obstructionism" had blocked Soviet efforts to reform the bloc and blunted East German moves for integration. At the same time, it established a solid precedent for an independent line within the tolerance levels of the Soviet Union.[54]

The precedent in economic matters was reinforced when frictions developed between Rumania and the USSR over proper party relations. In April 1964, Party First Secretary, Gheorghiu-Dej, announced Rumania's "declaration of independence" by defending its right to national autonomy and equality within the socialist commonwealth and insisting that other parties refrain from interference in its internal affairs. Bucharest then accentuated the Soviets' dispute with China as a means of gaining greater leverage in its bid to secure general acceptance of a more satisfactory formula for the behavior of one party to another. From 1964 until the Chinese Cultural Revolution, when the Soviet Union was largely on the defensive throughout the world against Peking's ideological offensive, Bucharest acted as a self-appointed mediator. Bucharest consistently opposed Soviet efforts to denounce Chinese heretical behavior on the grounds that efforts to establish ideological and political norms were inconsistent with the sovereignty and equality of members of the socialist commonwealth. During the peak of Rumania's bid to triangularize its involvement in the Sino-Soviet dispute, Moscow appeared to be both irritated and constrained. Bucharest succeeded in establishing its claims to a special position within the commonwealth based on conservative socialist domestic policies, loyalty to the Warsaw Pact, and autonomy in foreign policy.

Tensions in relations between the Soviet Union and Rumania reached a new dimension when security and foreign policy issues were added to those of economic and party affairs. When Brezhnev called for an all-European security conference at the March 1966 Soviet Party Congress, the Rumanians appeared surprised. The program for a new collective security arrangement encompassing both halves of Europe was not new, but the timing and seeming urgency were. It represented one of the first diplomatic initiatives of the Brezhnev regime and focused specifically on Moscow's primary European problem: the German question and Bonn's threat to continental security. Rumanian party leader Nicolai Ceaucescu challenged the Soviet proposal, claiming that military pacts were an "anachronism" in contemporary international relations and calling for the simultaneous dissolution of the opposing military alliances.[55] The new Soviet initiative was too abrupt and the Rumanian leadership remained obdurate: It insisted on comprehensive Pact-wide deliberations of the issues before pursuing the matter with the West. Consequently two unprecedented ministerial-level Pact meetings, lasting nearly a full month, were convened in Moscow to consider the problem of defense, the nature of the security threat, and East-West relations.[56]

There were several probable reasons for Rumania's surprise at the new Soviet European initiatives. Its successful engagement in the Sino-Soviet dispute may have led to "heady" assessments that its new relationship with the communist giants would preclude encroachments by either power on its hard-fought for autonomy. The ebullient Khrushchev had created a political style that tainted Brezhnev as a pale unadventurous leader, dedicated to the preservation of existing holdings, rather than to the development of new policy options. The West was responding positively to the changing atmosphere on the German question that had forced the Soviets and the other East Europeans onto the defensive. Finally, the distinct change in Moscow's East European policy between 1964 and 1966 was not yet apparent; indeed it was a period marked by a noticeable lack of Soviet policy.

The agenda for the extraordinary sessions of the Warsaw Pact's defense and foreign ministers in Moscow was sweeping. It included earlier Soviet proposals for strengthening the Pact's institutional structure, accelerating the rate of force modernization in Eastern Europe, and a demonstration at the missile site at Semipalatinsk on the latest Soviet ICBMs. It now seems certain that the assembled ministers were informed that technological breakthroughs had occurred, especially in the large-scale production of liquid propellants that would permit Moscow to launch an ICBM construction program designed to achieve parity with the United States in such components of strategic weaponry as missile throw-weight. The Soviets reportedly argued that the planned mass production of the new SS-9 and SS-11 ICBM and expected American recognition of its stature as a strategic equal would provide the Pact for the first time since the postwar period with sufficient leverage to force a European settlement in a favorable direction. Strengthened military postures and political solidarity throughout the Pact, however, were essential to improve the East Europeans' bargaining position.

Rumania objected to all of the Soviet proposals, except that for conducting arms limitations negotiations. It responded that a major increase in Soviet strategic power would be observed by the United States and would merely trigger a new round in arms competition that the Soviets might lose, as they had in the past, and create tensions rather than induce conciliation. Bucharest rejected demands for extending the Pact's structure and called first for a genuine manifestation of the equality of the smaller members in decision-making. It complained that it could not afford procurement costs for new weapons at that time. To underscore its earlier plea for the dissolution of both alliances, it asked for voluntary Soviet reductions in troops stationed abroad and petitioned the other members to suspend payments for the costs of stationing Soviet troops in Eastern Europe (Rumania formally withdrew from the Pact's burden-sharing arrangement the following February). Rumania was not challenging the legality but the morality of garrisoning Soviet units in Eastern Europe and its opposition to Soviet military planning reached a crescendo when the foreign ministers met to discuss the political aspects of Moscow's proposed security conference.

In order to provide the political solidarity desired for the Pact, the Soviets sought a consensus on the sources of European instability, namely, a mutual denunciation of West German revanchism as the main threat to European peace. Rumania agreed only to a moderate wording that would permit continued probing for further openings in Bonn. East Germany insisted on an unqualified condemnation as the cement for cohesion and a display of loyalty to the collective cause. Rumania replied that the stalemate in Europe stemmed from the indecision by both sides about whether to risk first political or military disengagement. (The West refused to deal with political matters when faced with a military confrontation, and the East rejected military reductions until after a political settlement had been reached, if even then.) If the deadlock was to be resolved, movement would have to be made by both sides on both political and military matters at the same time. The exchanges with the East Germans became so bitter that Rumania walked out of one session and refused to participate further until Breszhnev personally provided assurance that it would not be expected to join Pact discussions on issues, such as

China, Israel, or Germany, where it would be forced into a minority position—a valuable precedent for Rumanian abstention of an increasing range of issues. Rumanian Foreign Minister Corneliu Monescu told reporters upon his return to Bucharest that he was pleased with the results of his two weeks of hard bargaining and Rumania's efforts toward *"bridge-building with the West."*[57]

A compromise was finally reached, embodied in a communiqué on July 8, 1966 issued by the Pact's Political Consultative Committee, known as the Bucharest Declaration. The Declaration was heralded throughout the Pact as the definitive statement of the members' positions. Indeed, for the first time, it presented a general statement of Pact demands and then itemized the respective members' complaints against the West. The main points were the identification of the sources of international tensions as German revanchism, American imperialism, and NATO militarism, a diluted formula that did not single out the FRG alone. The preconditions for a lasting peace in Europe were Bonn's recognition of the GDR and the existing European boundaries and renunciation of all territorial claims and interest in acquiring nuclear weapons. The citation of individual positions included the Rumanian demands for international respect for national sovereignty, the principle of non-interference in domestic affairs, the necessity of strengthening relations among states regardless of their political systems, and the abrogation of military blocs.

The Declaration was a new high point in the East Europeans' agreement about a common German policy. But the Rumanian caveat was an important reservation that its allies seriously misperceived. Bucharest viewed the Pact's chorusing on the German threat as a dangerous extension of Soviet hegemony, especially if the solution of national grievance against Bonn would render Pact members even more indebted to Moscow. If the individual members could not act bilaterally to settle their differences with the Federal Republic, Rumania was determined to pursue a course that would promote its goal of advancing both military and political détente, especially against the "main threat" to European security.

Prior to the confrontation with the Soviets and East Germans, Rumania explored the prospects for opening diplomatic relations with Bonn during a February 1966 visit of a trade delegation to the FRG, followed by tours by the Rumanian foreign trade minister in May and the West German economics minister in September. The fall of the Erhard government in October delayed the schedule, indicating that Bucharest's commitment to the Pact Declaration had been made with severe qualifications. The new Grand Coalition promptly informed Moscow in mid-December that it intended to send delegations to Hungary and Czechoslovakia to explore diplomatic relations, suggesting that the momentum for accommodation was gaining on both sides.[58]

In January 1967 Rumania became the first Pact country, besides the Soviet Union, to establish full diplomatic relations with the Federal Republic. Rumania's action created in effect a two-Germanys policy that broke the Pact's agreement on the source and nature of the common threat and precipitated the worst political crisis for the Pact since 1956. The Bucharest Declaration was intended to be a demonstration of solidarity and the guidelines for future political planning by the Pact nations that could counter Bonn's "opening to the East." Rumanian adoption of a two-Germanys policy, however, denied the Pact the consensus upon which effective implementation of the Declaration was based.[59]

Rumania replied to the unanimous criticism from its allies that its two-Germanys policy complemented Pact goals of promoting regional security through relaxing tensions and reducing Bonn's intransigence toward Eastern Europe. Accepting diplomatic relations with Rumania, an ally to the GDR, had forced the Federal Republic to endorse the two-Germanys standard and compromised its own Hallstein Doctrine. Indeed, this was Bonn's first step away from its policy of claiming exclusive authority for Germany that could be argued implied acceptance of the equality of the two Germanys. Bucharest concluded that there were both "good and bad" West Germans (the "constructive" forces in the SPD and FDP and the "reactionary" elements in the CDU and NDP), and the Pact should follow Rumania's lead in encouraging the West Germans to shift their priorities from reunification to normalization.[60] Rumania was forced to maintain its two-Germanys policy for nearly two years, isolating itself from all Pact meetings dealing with this subject.

The degree of apparent surprise registered by the Soviets and the other Pact members over Rumania's "defection" is difficult to understand, especially since the West Germans informed Moscow in advance of their intentions to exchange ambassadors. Moscow's seeming reticence to react more decisively against Bucharest may have resulted from uncertainty about an appropriate course that would appease East Germany without further alienating Rumania. On February 8, within one month of Bucharest's independent action, the Pact foreign ministers met without Rumania to devise a common position against both Bucharest and Bonn. The FRG's "enticement" of Rumania was denounced as tactics to undermine Pact solidarity rather than a demonstration of German adjustment toward the East as a whole.[61]

The majority, led by East Germany, formulated three basic countermoves. A polemical campaign was launched at the outset to explain the correct interpretation of the Bucharest Declaration and to expose Rumanian errors.[62] Second, the GDR gained unanimous endorsement for its own inverted Hallstein Doctrine, known as the Ulbricht Doctrine and first proposed at the SED Central Committee plenum on December 15, 1966. The new policy required Bonn's recognition of the GDR as the precondition for establishing diplomatic relations by the FRG with any other Pact member. Finally the GDR gained acceptance of a scheme for enhancing its security and equality within the Pact through the conclusion of a series of bilateral mutual defense treaties with all other Pact members. (The initial series had been negotiated in the postwar era and was superceded in principle by the provisions of the Warsaw Pact; the GDR had only one such accord, with the USSR). The East Europeans agreed to the renegotiation of the redundant pacts primarily because they tended to reinforce the territorial status quo. Moscow showed interest because a series of accords among all members would provide an additional legal basis for military cooperation in the event the Warsaw Pact Treaty was ever abrogated or that one or more members chose to refrain from a military contingency. All agreed that the accords would demonstrate their cohesion and thereby improve their negotiating position vis-à-vis the West Germans.

During the following six months, East Berlin negotiated bilateral treaties with Poland, Czechoslovakia, Hungary, and Bulgaria. The provisions stressed the existence of two German states, the inviolability of existing borders, the presence of West Berlin on East German territory, and mutual aid in the event of military aggression—standard fare for the GDR and its allies. The exception remained Rumania which refused to negotiate an agreement with East Berlin on terms that might jeopardize the even-handedness of its two-Germanys policy. Equally important, since the series included all Pact members, the talks Rumania held with the Soviets became the keystone for Bucharest's negotiations with its other allies, especially East Germany. The original Soviet-Rumanian Treaty, signed on February 4, 1948, contained three provisions essential to the renewed negotiations: the nature of the obligatory consultations, the automatically binding nature of the commitments, and the agreement to take joint actions to obviate any German threat. The Rumanians claimed that the Soviets violated the first provision during the Cuban Missile Crisis and endangered their national security. They wanted iron-clad guarantees for full consultations in the future, which the Soviets were reluctant to provide. However, the Rumanians also sought to increase the flexibility in the automacity of their obligations, while preserving the rigidity of Soviet commitments. Yet the Rumanians could not accept a 20-year treaty obligation that identified the West Germans as the chief threat. The talks were conducted until 1970, when a bilateral treaty was also signed with the GDR.

These obdurate delays by Bucharest underscored its continuing determination to establish a special status for itself and emphasized the lingering bitterness between Rumania and East Germany that afflicted the Pact's effectiveness. Rumania had succesfully defied Soviet leadership on the German question; an issue of prime concern for the Pact as a body and of vital importance for the Northern Tier members. Rumanian defiance had far-reaching implications for the formation of future East German foreign policy. Soviet "tolerance levels" on critical matters had been systematically probed and apparently roughly defined. Paradoxically, Ulbricht now perceived this new outline of constraints on Soviet behavior as new latitudes within which the GDR could pursue its own national objectives.

CREATING AN ATMOSPHERE FOR DIALOGUE

While the Rumanian two-Germanys initiative broke the deadlock over political versus military accommodation, the principle communist actors in the resolution of the German problem remained the GDR and the Soviet Union. Adjustments in their attitudes similar to those that were made by West Germany were necessary to create an atmosphere for productive dialogue.

By maintaining the Wall, the GDR publicly acknowledged its inability to insure domestic tranquility or gain international recognition of the legitimacy of its rule without its allies' support. But in the two years prior to the Czechoslovak crisis, East Berlin demonstrated both an increasingly assertive, yet still defensive posture.

In 1965, East Berlin intervened to force the cancellation of an invitation to the West German Catholic Church by the Polish Church to participate in celebrations of the millennium of Catholicism in Poland. After initially agreeing in 1966, it later cancelled a proposed exchange between East and West German youth groups. In the exchange of letters from 1966 to 1967 between the two governments and between the SPD and SED, East Berlin launched a campaign claiming that there was a renewed need to form an alliance between working classes in both parts of Germany. The GDR finally refused to exchange speakers, allegedly because of fears that Bonn could not insure their safety, yet both sides continued to communicate via the news media. The formal correspondence ended in 1967 when the GDR submitted a draft treaty that was intended to normalize and legalize relations between two fully sovereign states. Ulbricht reacted to Erhard's "opening" with a counteroffensive of his own. In a series of notes to the UN Secretary General and all European governments, he argued that reunification was not an ethnic but a social and class question. To offset Bonn's attempted isolation maneuver, he proposed the creation of a confederation of the two German states that would be based on workers' organizations in both states requiring social changes in the West such as the abolition of "monopolies," among other things. Furthermore, when Western Europe recognized the GDR, Ulbricht stated that both Germanys should renounce the acquisition of nuclear weapons, disarm, and seek security through the guarantees of a pan-European treaty arrangement. Ulbricht's tactic was completely unrealistic, but not unfamiliar, and was to be frequently repeated. East Berlin's objective was to compel Bonn to recognize the GDR and then reconcile itself to the existence of a separate, communist state.

East Germany was equally assertive in the east. It had reacted vigorously to the Rumanian challenge, but it also quickly perceived the potential danger of the Czechoslovak reforms and became the prime-mover in organizing the Warsaw Pact countries, minus Rumania, into a cohesive opposition to Dubeck at a summit conference in March 1968 at Dresden. The five Pact countries based their complaints on two pillars of orthodoxy: the fundamentalists' grievances against wholesale revisionism and the security threat posed by West German "revanchism." The Federal Republic's territorial claims and political ambitions in Eastern Europe were widely known and were now regarded as a source of sedition against Czechoslovakia. Prague's alleged inability to defend itself against the allurement of Western liberalism in the forms of massive West German credits and favorable trade terms were cited as justification for external intervention. Implicit in the fundamentalists' attack against the FRG was an element of retribution for

participating in Rumania's two-Germanys policy and undermining the Pact's position toward the West. Bonn had succeeded in making political inroads into Eastern Europe and the
Pact had been able to take only defensive, reactive measures,
a clear danger to East Germany's viability.

The GDR also demonstrated modest affronts to the Soviet
Union. Shortly after the invasion of Czechoslovakia, a confrontation with Moscow was actually provoked by East Berlin.
The two had agreed to approach Bonn about a possible agreement for passes through the Wall for West Berliners in exchange for transferring the election of the federal president
from West Berlin to another city. Soon after the initial understanding, the GDR withdrew its commitment, embarrassing
the Soviet Union by forcing it also to recant in support of its
ally, even though at that time, it was promoting a wide range of
negotiations with Bonn. Also during the same period the GDR
made the unprecedented move of formally granting the East
Berlin deputies the right to participate fully in the Volks-
kammer (parliament), an explicit violation of the Four-Power
agreements outlining the special status of Berlin that had been
honored by the USSR and still is by the Western Allies.
Further, the resumption of periodic harrassment of traffic
along the autobahns had the markings of being designed by
East Berlin to promote its own aims. Finally, after the invasion, an international conference was convened to commem-
orate the fiftieth anniversary of the Comintern. (The date was
inaccurate, indicating that there were probably other motives
for the gathering.) The Soviets formally condemned the Stalinist denunciation of the German SPD as the chief enemy of
communism and admonished the East European representatives to pursue a policy of support for the SPD as the most
plausible means of curbing rightist German tendencies. Ulbricht, the highest ranking non-Soviet present, marked his dis-
pleasure by a premature departure.[63]

However modest, such manifestations of self-assertion were
a break with traditional East German behavior. Indeed East
Berlin was developing a foreign policy, however negative, of its
own. Thus an important side effect of confrontation between

Bucharest, East Berlin, and Moscow over the two-Germanys policy and Rumania's special status within the Pact was that it provided the precedent and motivation for an increasingly independent, flexible, and active East German foreign policy. To counter Rumanian self-assertion required energetic and original counterefforts by the East Germans. By 1969, the GDR had concluded that it had developed sufficient political strength to inhibit major adjustments with the West at its expense, such as Khrushchev threatened to do in 1964.

On the Soviet side, East-West German problems were perceived within the framework of larger great-power relations. After early 1966, there was a renewed focus on Soviet European policy centered on security matters. Moscow accepted in principle a West German draft declaration drawn up in February 1967 that renounced the use of force between the two states. Bonn stated it was prepared to conclude similar agreements with all East European countries, including the GDR. Negotiations on the terms continued for nearly one and a half years before Moscow published several notes during the Prague crisis and the exchange was suspended.[64] The Soviet conditions for such an accord had been mentioned before, but seldom as a package agreement for serious negotiations. They included FRG renunciation of access to nuclear weapons, FRG recognition of West Berlin as a special political entity, FRG invalidation of the 1938 Munich Agreement, *ab initio*, FRG recognition of the inviolability of existing European borders, and FRG commitment to normalize relations with the GDR.[65] To pressure Bonn during these exchanges, Moscow reopened its formerly muted claims to the right of unilateral intervention in West German domestic affairs, under Articles 53 and 107 of the UN Charter, the so-called "enemy state" provisions, if it judged Bonn's actions and policies detrimental to international peace. The most frequently mentioned provocations were the rise of militarism and neo-Nazism.[66]

When Bonn was forced by the Soviet leak to publish the entire diplomatic exchange, it created a public uproar, only barely overshadowed by events in Prague. The government replied that no commitments had been made; only a dialogue had been conducted that had already produced modest dividends in the area of trade. (The Soviets had launched a major commercial campaign in West Germany and trade between the two countries increased 38 percent in 1968 to a total of $567 million.) Nonetheless, the negative public reactions over conditions that resembled a quasi-peace treaty, coupled with embarrassment over the Prague invasion, apparently convinced Moscow that the dialogue should be reopened as soon as possible and that the soviets would have to be more accommodating with West German interests.

There were more general reasons for the modification of the East German and Soviet positions. The erection of the Wall largely stemmed the flow of refugees and stabilized the East German labor force, especially among professional personnel, recent university graduates, and skilled workers. The economic reforms and reorganization of 1963 eased the GDR past the recession that plagued all socialist countries in the mid-1960s. By the late 1960s, the GDR's new prosperity tended to reinforce social stability, giving the SED leadership reassurance that, while not loved, they were respected in both East and West. Slowly developing confidence was no substitute for genuine legitimacy, but it provided the basis for both the evolution of an exploratory yet defensive policy toward the FRG and a more assertive and demanding stance among its allies.

The factors that influenced the modest alteration in Soviet policy are more numerous, and more difficult to rank in the order of their importance. A simplistic itemization of those factors would include (1) the change in Kremlin leadership, (2) the temporary elimination of the Chinese challenge, (3) the heavy American engagement in Vietnam and willingness to negotiate on other issues—"bridge-building," (4) modest advances at the Geneva disarmament talks, such as the Limited Nuclear Test Ban Treaty, and the draft Nuclear Nonproliferation Treaty, (5) French flirtation with Moscow's policy interests, (6) the economic necessity for broader Western commercial contacts, and (7) the growing responsiveness of the main West German parties. These factors combined to provide the Soviet leadership the confidence that they could moderate the feud between East Germany and Rumania, contain the Prague "inflammation," and still seek an adjustment in Germany without jeopardizing Soviet interests.

To achieve the priority aim of the legitimization of communist rule in Eastern Europe, the new leadership placed increasing emphasis on resolving national grievances against West Germany rather than the former almost exclusive reliance on security measures.

Chapter III

Advent and Conclusion of Serious Bargaining

To the surprise of many observers the tone in East-West European relations changed noticeably after the Prague crisis. The German threat had failed to materialize; indeed, Bonn had prudently suspended contacts with Prague. The Czechoslovak renaissance continued for nearly nine months, after the permanent installation of Soviet garrisons, indicating that the alleged German threat was only the pretext for the invasion. This demonstrated the dubious nature of the German danger and its limited utility as an instrument for inducing public support and for promoting national interests. It now appears that Moscow recognized soon after the invasion that the use of the German threat had miscarried and took a series of unilateral steps to reopen the dialogue with Bonn (these unilateral rather than multilateral approaches, such as the Karlovy Vary conference, suggests that the Soviets were determined to promote contacts with the FRG regardless of East German opposition).

On October 8, 1968, a week before the signing of the treaty legalizing the garrisoning of Soviet troops in Czechoslovakia, foreign ministers Gromyko and Brandt met in New York and agreed to suspend polemics on Soviet rights for intervention either under the "enemy state" clause or the doctrine of "limited sovereignty" and to explore areas of common interest instead. Bonn also implicitly agreed to accept Soviet terms for its further involvement in East Europe: no additional inroads or

[51]

changes in the diplomatic status quo were to be launched without Soviet endorsement or, preferably, without the conclusion of a general regional agreement between the Soviet Union and the FRG. Renewed talks were opened in earnest after Christmas over the issue of West German accession to the NPT Treaty. Bonn insisted upon a Soviet clarification of its right to intervention under the UN Charter before an FRG assignation could be expected. Moscow verbally dropped its claims, removing the main obstacle to FRG endorsement of the treaty.

In March 1969, Soviet Ambassador Semyon Tsarapkin took the unprecedent measure of formally briefing the West German Chancellor on the recent clashes with the Chinese on the Ussuri River. While this may have been intended to dissuade the FRG and the United States from interpreting the incidents as a manifestation of Soviet weakness against Chinese provocation, West German sources concluded that it was also a signal to East Berlin that it could no longer employ the tactic of siding with China to pressure the USSR.[67] (At that time the GDR was conducting a major polemical campaign against Bonn for proposing to hold the presidential elections in West Berlin, an issue largely ignored by the Soviets.)

In a significant gesture, a communiqué was issued in March 1969 by the Pact's Political Consultative Committee. It dropped the customary vindicative denunciation of West Germany as the main threat to European stability and instead amplified the call for a European security conference amid informal asides that the Pact's position was subject to negotiation. Equally important, the communiqué did not demand FRG legal recognition of the GDR as a precondition for convening the gathering, indicating that the Ulbricht Doctrine had lost its former authority, if it had not yet been completely abandoned. These moves at East Berlin's expense brought the Soviet position to the point that commonality of interest with the FRG began to emerge on several issues, such as the reopening of the dialogue and placing it on a formal basis. Tsarapkin requested that Chancellor Kiesinger send a personal envoy to Moscow to test the climate. Rudolf Heizler, a close confidant, reported on his return that "the Soviet Union is seeking a dialogue with the

Federal Republic; it is clearly interested in a reconciliation and an understanding with Bonn."[68]

There were negotiations also underway on related matters that had the positive effect of contributing to a favorable atmosphere. Lufthansa and Aeroflot opened talks on reciprocal air flight rights and discussions began on an unprecedented commercial transaction totaling over $400 million, whereby West German large-diameter steel pipe would be exchanged for Soviet natural gas. On May 17, Poland's party chief Gomulka endorsed the new line, a break with its former policy of unquestioned support for the GDR position.[69] (At a press conference two days later, Brandt termed Gomulka's offer for official talks with Bonn "remarkable.")[70] On July 10, Foreign Minister Gromyko told the Supreme Soviet that a turning point had been reached in Soviet relations with the Federal Republic.[71] Brandt stated on the same day that relations between the two states were approaching normalcy.[72] Finally on September 12, Moscow accepted the West German terms for opening formal talks on a treaty for the renunciation of the use of force. According to Brandt, Bonn agreed to exchange pledges of nonaggression with the GDR that would be regarded as binding as treaties under international law.[73] The Soviets neither accepted nor rejected these reservations, but they indicated their willingness to open talks—a cautious formula intended not to damage the SPD chances during the forthcoming national elections. Thus, in just over one year after the invasion of Czechoslovakia, the Soviets had virtually overcome the negative effects of their intervention and succeeded in restoring the momentum of their reconciliation with Bonn by expanding the number of issues under consideration to the point that the mere volume had a self-perpetuating affect. This campaign gradually vindicated the Rumanian two-Germanys policy and slowly forced the GDR from its intransigent position.

The national West German election in September 1969 assumed a historic dimension as the various platforms became public. It obviously would be too simplistic to characterize West German politics as polarized between rival positions. Each of the four contending parties were divided on ideological differences and personalities. The April 1969 SPD party conference seized the initiative. Record prosperity, declining influence of refugee groups, and a change in voter attitudes toward reconciliation with the East seemed to justify an assertive campaign focusing heavily on *Ostpolitik*. For example, in June 1967, 19 percent of those interviewed favored recognition of the Oder-Neisse border and 51 percent opposed. Yet 50 percent favored recognition of the line if German reunification could be achieved, while 25 percent did not. But by the end of 1969, 74 percent favored official talks with the GDR, and over 50 percent accepted formal recognition of the GDR and renunciation of the "lost territories," that is, recognition of the Oder-Neisse.[74] Under these circumstances, a more flexible policy seemed more attractive to a majority of the SPD delegates.

The CDU and CSU appeared constrained by two overriding considerations. On the one hand, they could not accept a change in the conceptualization of the German state, either as a modification of earlier norms or the inclusion of an unrepresentative government as a separate entity within a single national unit. The objective of Germany as a single political entity with compatible, if not common, institutions must govern long-range policy. On the other hand, they were compelled to consider the ultranationalistic demands made by the NPD May Party Congress: "No recognition of territorial adjustments or acceptance of the stolen territories." Thus the CDU/CSU feared being "passed on the right" and adopted a strongly conservative platform on Eastern problems that allowed the SPD to focus on its *Ostpolitik* as a main thrust of its campaign. The results of the elections were a decline of 1.5 percent for the CDU but a retention with the CSU of its plurality and a sharp 3.4 percent rise for the SPD to 42.7 percent and a drop of 3.7 percent for the FDP to only 5.8 percent. A coalition was formed between the SPD and the FDP that had a bare 12-vote majority in the *Bundestag*. Since the government primarily had based its campaign on *Ostpolitik* and not on domestic issues such as those of law and order, it concluded that the results were a clear electoral mandate to seek an accommodation with the USSR, the GDR, and Eastern Europe.

OPENING NEGOTIATING ROUNDS

In Brandt's speech to the *Bundestag* on October 28, 1969 he reviewed the relationship of West Germany to East Europe and advanced the new government's position on all issues. With East Germany, he offered to discuss outstanding differences on the basis of equality (a GDR demand) that might lead to contractual accords below the level of treaties (the West German stand). He formally restated the SPD position that Bonn was now prepared to accept a formula for the existence of two German states within one nation, but could never agree to the presence of two alien German states. The new government was prepared to negotiate nonaggression pacts or renunciation of force agreements with all Warsaw Pact members, including the GDR. But accords with the GDR would have the binding qualities of treaties, without their political implications. Such pacts would acknowledge the territorial integrity of the signators.[75]

Within several weeks, Brandt responded on other issues sponsored by East Europe. He strongly supported the call for a European security conference, with the proviso that sufficient progress was made first between the two Germanys in resolving their differences. There would be little hope that the two halves of Europe could settle outstanding problems if the Germans were unable to do so. (This was the first example of Brandt's formal injection of the principle of *junktim*: linking consideration of one issue with progress on a related matter.) The new government also announced its qualified preparedness to drop opposition to recognition of the GDR by third states, provided East Berlin demonstrated genuine moves toward improving inner-German cooperation and that third states were not stampeded into "premature actions."

On the issue of the NPT, the Soviet Union provided Bonn with a formal note on November 9 accepting the principle that the FRG should have uninhibited access to peaceful use of nuclear energy. West German access to nuclear weapons and nuclear materials had developed into a major controversy. Bonn maintained that it had renounced, under its treaty obligations with its Western allies, any interest in possessing nuclear weapons. Furthermore, it was the only country in the world which voluntarily opened its defense industries to international inspection by the Arms Control Agency of the West European Union (WEU) to insure compliance. This was an adequate guarantee. However, the FRG had the right and responsibility to participate in the nuclear defense of the West under proper NATO authorization until there were adequate disarmament accords. Finally, the FRG, like any other state, had the right to employ nuclear energy for peaceful purposes; to deny this right would impose blatant discrimination.

On the other side, the Soviets combined the regulation of military and industrial applications of nuclear power into the same lethal category. They charged that the WEU inspection unit was operated by Bonn's allies, not its adversaries, and was hardly reliable. On the issue of West German access to tactical nuclear weapons, the procedures to prevent the transfer of weapons or their technology might satisfy the United States but not the Soviets. Operational requirements necessitated that American procedures be as simple as possible to facilitate timely military employment and not necessarily as secure as possible to preclude unauthorized use or disclosure; and therefore were subject to Soviet criticism. Finally, Western German peaceful uses of nuclear energy were inspected only by EURA-TOM, an organization within the Common Market and therefore partial to West German industrial interests. Moscow demanded that all FRG nuclear reactors be placed under the safeguards supervision of the International Atomic Energy Agency (IAEA).

Bonn's response was to insist on the separation of the military and peaceful applications and to argue that while the aim of NPT was to prevent the spread of nuclear capabilities, control procedures within the various alliances were beyond the treaty's purview. On safeguards for peaceful uses, Bonn refused to submit to IAEA inspections because of the dangers of industrial espionage by members of a worldwide organization. The Soviet note opened the way for West German as-signation of the NPT on November 28 and submission of a formal proposal for talks on a renunciation of the use of force treaty that commenced on December 7. From the West German perspective, a successful conclusion of such an accord would guarantee the forfeiture of Moscow's alleged right of intervention under the UN provisions and would promote both political engagement and military disengagement. From the Soviet standpoint, FRG endorsement of a nonaggression treaty would register Bonn's de facto acceptance of the status quo in Eastern Europe by the renunciation of nuclear force for the recovery of the last territories. (There was evidence at that time that the Soviets envisioned the culmination of its European security campaign as the conclusion of a series of bilateral renunciations of force treaties between the FRG and the East Europeans, consecrated by a multilaterial conference.)[76]

At a Pact summit meeting on December 3, 1969 German policy was modified. All seven members concluded that their respective bargaining positions on European matters could best be served by formulating a coordinated but individual stance vis-à-vis Bonn. It was agreed that sufficient flexibility had been demonstrated by the FRG to permit each member to pursue settlement of its respective problems with Bonn on a bilateral basis—allowing a natural division of labor first envisioned in the 1966 Bucharest Declaration. (This 1969 decision focusing on individual national grievances also may have been a consequence of dissent over Soviet involvement in the Middle East and its impact on Eastern Europe, especially on Czechoslovakia and Poland. It added to the compartmentalization of the interests of these states into those of "Little Europeans" that has remained fixed since then, allowing Moscow greater freedom of action on the global stage.)[77] After the meeting each member issued a formal statement of its bargaining expectations vis-à-vis Bonn, indicating that a particularist approach was now acceptable.[78]

Bonn responded positively. On January 14 in his state of the nation address, Brandt called for talks between the two Germanys based on complete equality with the aim of providing assurances that neither would attempt to alter the existing social structures of the other state. He reiterated his thesis that the two states should exist in one nation and voiced continued support for Four-Power responsibilities for the status of Berlin and Germany as a whole, and envisioned national unity only within the context of a general European peace order.[79]

Thus within 100 days, the new FRG coalition made major concessions toward the GDR and East Europeans' preconditions for negotiations. To summarize these positions, the Warsaw Pact countries traditionally had raised eight specific demands for normalization of relations: (1) legal recognition of the GDR, (2) abrogation of the Hallstein Doctrine and the concept of exclusive authority for German interests, (3) recognition of the existing East European borders and the renunciation of German territorial claims, (4) rejection of any ambitions for the possession of nuclear weapons, (5) support for general disarmament proposals, (6) formal acceptance of the principle that the Munich Agreement was null and void *ab initio*, (7) agreement that West Berlin was an independent political entity, and (8) proscription of the "neo-Nazi" NPD.

By 1970 the Brandt government had responded in the following manner. It continued to withhold legal recognition of the GDR but accepted its existence; also the former policy of reunification was superseded by normalization. It abandoned the Hallstein Doctrine of exclusive responsibility for German interests; and a new formula providing for the sanctity of the Oder-Neisse had been recommended as the basis for negotiations. The government attempted to reduce formal pact reservations about West German aspirations for nuclear weapons by signing the NPT. It agreed to participate in negotiations on a treaty for the mutual renunciation of force as a positive contribution to arms limitations. It developed new formula for renouncing the Munich Agreement as illegal and immoral but shelved it pending the conclusion of the more urgent accords. It continued to give full support for the Four Powers in Berlin and Germany, a central feature of *Ostpolitik*. The NPD had been reduced to political insignificance by the September elections and therefore was conveniently removed from further policy considerations.

This mutual responsiveness generated a favorable atmosphere conducive to negotiations. It became clear only belatedly that the Soviets had excessively ambitious expectations for the negotiations. The West German opposition leaked the so-called "Bahr Papers" to the press which revealed that the original Soviet proposals and subsequent FRG responses covered the entire spectrum of East European-West German grievances. The document was to guarantee Bonn's acceptance of the existing realities in Eastern Europe by the abrogation of those interests, and claims that could challenge the present status quo. Its legal commitment to the status quo was to enhance stability, security, and legitimacy in East Europe and thereby reinforce the Soviet terms for a final peace treaty ending World War II. CDU opposition and allied intervention dissuaded Bonn from pursuing the broader accord.

On June 7, the Brandt government opened formal negotiations with the Soviets along guidelines that reduced the intended provisions from those of a comprehensive peace treaty. They went, however, beyond those of a mere renunciation force agreement. The West German negotiating principles stated that relations between the two states should be based on the renunciation of force and the threat of using force. Also, the Four-Power talks on Berlin were to insure continuing close ties and unhampered access between the FRG and West Berlin. The agreement would not affect the German peoples' right of self-determination. Finally, the accords with all Pact members should be considered as a package, but they would not affect the provisions of the West German Constitution which specifically calls for reunification.[80]

The accord, commonly known as the Soviet-West German Normalization Treaty, was signed on August 12, 1970. Article 1 provided for movement toward normalization of relations among European states based on the existing situation in this region. Article 2 called for the renunciation of force or the threatened use of force. Article 3 specified the mutual recognition of present frontiers and the renunciation of all territorial claims, which was accompanied by a West German caveat about a final settlement of the German problem. The treaty, therefore, included the German right to self-determination and the establishment of definitive borders by a final peace treaty within the context of either an inner-German or an overall European settlement. Finally, Article 4 stated that the treaty did not impair the provisions of any multilateral or bilateral commitments of either party, including (in separate letters) the Four Powers' responsibilities for Germany and Berlin.[81]

The proponents in the SPD of the treaty claimed that it was a major contribution to European détente, for the renunciation of force would be a significant constraint on Soviet behavior. The FRG was no longer the "main threat" to European stability and was granted a degree of respectability commensurate with that of other Western powers. The way was now opened to improved relations with other Pact nations. The principle of self-determination and Allied responsibilities had been upheld and clarified. No commitments were made on negotiations with the GDR, but Moscow was obliged to conclude the Berlin negotiations. Finally, new commercial opportunities could be expected.

In Bundestag debates the opposition countered these expectations by charging that the treaty relinquished 40,000 square miles of territory (one quarter of 1938 Germany) without provisions for the right of refugees to return to appropriate reparations. Bonn had lost its leverage on the borders issues and any revisions now were remote. Acceptance of the status quo also implied acquiescence of Soviet hegemony over Eastern Europe and the application of the Brezhnev doctrine of "limited sovereignty." The East Europeans, including the East Germans, had now lost valuable latitude for increasing their options against Soviet centralism. Finally, there were no indications that the Soviets were sincere in pursuing negotiations on military disengagement, the corollary to political détente, implying that Moscow was achieving its political objectives, while the West was still faced with a military confrontation.[82]

Moscow was denied its maximum aim of a formalized state of peace, but it did achieve important intermediate goals. It had reduced the German threat, without diminishing the urgency for collective security against the imperialist West. To the contrary, breaking West German claims in the East reduced East European grievances against the FRG and contributed to re-

gional stability. Yet the provisions were only a marginal constraint against the insulation of Pact members from Western
ideological influence. This was a central motive behind the
Soviet's desire to promote a conference on European security.

The Polish-West German Treaty was signed in November
1970.[83] The central provisions were the recognition of the Oder-
Neisse border and the renunciation of German territorial
claims beyond that line. The Poles were concerned that the
FRG's claims to exclusive representation posed a continual
challenge to their territorial integrity and that a reunited Germany could actually threaten its borders. The Poles insisted on
and gained West German acceptance of the concept of inviolability of frontiers, and the renunciation of territorial claims. In
accompanying Letters, however, Bonn effectively tied the final
boundary delineation to the allied powers' responsibilities
under Chapter IX of the Decisions of the Potsdam Conference
which deferred the issue to a final peace conference. Bonn's
renunciation of its territorial claims of lands under present
Polish sovereignty was also accompanied by the caveat that
final endorsement of the "Polish-administered German Territories" was to remain a provision of a general peace treaty or
a European settlement. In a commercial accord, signed on
October 15, Bonn agreed to provide an annual credit of DM
500 million over five years. The Poles then agreed to the repa-
triation of ethnic Germans to the FRG (the definition of ethnic-
ity and familial ties remain major obstacles). In conjunction
with the signing of the "normalization" treaty, Poland agreed
to establish full diplomatic relations.

Again the proponents claimed that the treaty granted only
de facto, not *de jure* recognition of the borders. It had not
ceded sovereignty to the Polish-administered territories; it had
merely renounced its desire for their restitution. The treaty was
subordinated to the Potsdam and Paris accords on the boundary question, and no amendments to the German constitution
were required. Bonn had reserved for itself the right to speak
only for itself not for a reunited Germany, the Allies, or an
integrated Europe.

The opposition countered that Poland could claim juridically that the provisions were binding on any successor government. Warsaw's declaratory statements clearly indicated the finality it attached to the boundary wording. The increased number of consultations between Moscow and the principal Pact members over such bilateral negotiations increased Soviet hegemony but did not necessarily contribute to the improvement in East-West relations. Finally, the trade-off of economic credit for the return of ethnic Germans both smacked of buying freedom where other means should have been used and would likely break down if there were persistent trade imbalances that would demoralize thousands of would-be immigrants.[84]

Acceptance of the substance of the Soviet objectives by the FRG and the Western Allies, but their rejection of the principles and implications of those aims, represented probably the first instance when East-West détente assumed the characteristics of mutual constraint. It was now presumed that the "era of negotiation" and initial acknowledgement of political and military equality was to be accompanied by mutually demonstrated constraints in exploiting opportunities for the exercise of influence competition. Both treaties achieved the minimal aims of all parties and the protection of their vital interests. The successful conclusion of these two negotiations added impetus to the "inner-German" contacts.

EAST-WEST GERMAN DIALOGUE

East Berlin apparently assessed the consequences of the summit meeting in December 1969 as detrimental to its interests and adopted a highly assertive posture. Foreign Minister Otto Winzer reported the conference results to the SED Central Committee and stated the GDR's terms for talks with Bonn in distinctly nonconciliatory tones. He wanted to reinforce the Ulbricht Doctrine, whereby the FRG would not be permitted even to *improve* relations with other Pact members until it first accepted relations with the GDR on the basis of international law (an attempt to establish a *junktim* of its own, but with the weakness of linking movement on GDR problems with progress on those of other states which would give Bonn new leverage).[85] Ulbricht told the Central Committee on December 13 that the GDR rejected the thesis of establishing two states in one nation and demanded full legal recognition as a precondition for conducting political talks. On December 18, Ulbricht sent a draft treaty similar to a version drawn up in 1967 to President Gustav Heinemann to serve as a basis for possible discussions.[86] Yet the GDR then demanded that renunciation of Bonn's commitment to NATO was essential. Later it insisted that only the Four-Power documents governed relations between the two states and that compliance with those provisions required abrogation of economic monopolies and militarism as prerequisites to normalization. In a New Year's statement, Ulbricht insisted on an exchange of ambassadors and later on the statutory cancellation of a lengthy list of "imperialistic" federal laws. The GDR also insisted that any future accords on technical matters, such as postal regulations, must be granted the status of international treaties. Finally, the GDR warned Bonn against holding further Bundestag committee meetings in West Berlin.[87]

Thus in less than one month, the GDR reacted against the growing trend within the Pact toward exploring accommodation by raising the stakes for discussions with Bonn to the highest, least acceptable terms in recent years. There may be several explanations for advocating such exorbitant maximum conditions. It may have been a gambit intended to force a FRG response in kind which would demonstrate that no change had occurred in West German policy. Also, it may have been a blocking action to preclude unilateral advantages gained by its allies at its expense. Or, it may have been a reflection that the GDR was simply out of tune with the changes in FRG policy that its allies had readily perceived. The new conditions were probably a result of all and therefore received no official response from West Germany and were simply ignored in Brandt's national address.

Accordingly, Ulbricht held his first news conference in nine years on January 15 and substantially modified the GDR public stance.[88] Former preconditions were extended to the status of final goals. Full recognition and Bonn's renunciation of its Western ties were to be the characteristics of normalization. During the intervening period, both states were to conduct themselves in accordance to the rules of international law: renunciation of force, respect for sovereign equality, and non-interference in internal affairs. He proposed holding talks with the FRG with an open agenda. This "clarification" was closer to the minimum positions of both the East Europeans and Bonn, and within hours the Chancellory announced that it would probe the GDR's intentions by proposing a schedule for the talks in a formal note.

Bonn suggested that initial discussions be held at the ministerial level. East Berlin replied on February 3 with a deliberate insult. It insisted upon a summit meeting in East Berlin to be held within two weeks and then refused to participate if the Chancellor traveled through West Berlin. After a month's delay and an unexpected visit to East Berlin by Gromyko a compromise was reached. Reciprocal meetings were to be held in Erfurt and Kassel.

On March 19, 1970 Brandt and Stoph met for the first time as heads of German states. Instead of an open agenda, as had been mutually suggested in public, Stoph attempted to steer the dialogue toward a commitment on the acceptability of the draft treaty sent to Heinemann in December, which would insure full and equal sovereignty of the two states and mutual respect for territorial integrity. Stoph also proposed acceptance of several additional points: a 50 percent reduction in defense budgets, full deliberation of issues connected with the "burial of all vestiges of World War II," including the settlement of the debts and reparations "owed" to the GDR (primarily by the USSR), amounting to claims of 100 billion marks ($23 billion).

All of the points presented by Stoph had been previously raised. But when cited as a total package, they appeared as a nonnegotiable obstacle. However, Brandt presented no new innovations. Indeed, the published materials suggest that he was more concerned with generating a cooperative atmosphere as an inducement to detailed negotiations, the opposite to the GDR aim of gaining agreement on substantive matters as a manifestation of a cooperative intent. Brandt reported to the Bundestag that the GDR had raised a number of unacceptable demands.[89]

In the interval between the two meetings, East Berlin reopened its polemical campaign against Brandt and Bonn, which was quieted only after another visit by Gromyko. Bonn replied by reinvoking the Hallstein Doctrine and successfully obstructing the GDR's membership application in the World Health Organization. In retaliation, East Berlin increased the transit tax 30 percent for goods enroute between the FRG and West Berlin.

In contrast with this deterioration in the relation between the two Germanys, there was a notable increase in West German contacts with other Pact members during the same period ranging from political talks with Bulgaria, to negotiations with Hungary for a long-term trade arrangement, to the separate trade and political discussions conducted with Poland and the Soviet Union. While these new contacts were often unique in their scope and substance, the accumulative effect was a major escalation in Bonn's diplomatic offensive in Eastern Europe and a clear indication of the sterility of its dialogue thus far with the GDR.

On May 21 the two leaders met again at Kassel, West Germany. Brandt made new concessions to the GDR by presenting a comprehensive list of 20 points as the basis for an overall settlement. In summary, they included acknowledgment of each other's independence, respect for borders, renunciation of the use of force, and exchange of plenipotentiaries. Brandt even implied that he might recognize the GDR if East Berlin accepted the 20 points and if an improvement in relations was warranted.[90] But Stoph remained even more intransigent than at Erfurt. He insisted that full recognition was the necessary precondition for negotiations of any of the proposed points. The talks ended in a complete impasse. The gulf between the two Germanys was indeed widening.

The Kassel meeting marked a turning point in Bonn's *Ostpolitik*. Bonn had promoted its contacts with the East in a piecemeal fashion. It had not developed a comprehensive program of expectations or a strategy for their attainment. *Ostpolitik* was intended to contribute to détente, which was seen as a condition not a process, as the Communists view it. Progress in the negotiation process, therefore, depended on the skills of the central figures, such as Willy Brandt and Egon Bahr, the state secretary conducting the negotiations, not on the precision of a grand design.

The 20 points represented a shift away from this amorphous approach. It registered a new awareness of the way the GDR perceived of a settlement and presented a detailed response by the FRG to the GDR draft treaty. But the 20 points that had been proposed failed to produce the desired results. Despite mounting pressure from its allies, East Berlin had become progressively more truculent. The Kassel summit meeting forced Bonn to reevaluate its interests in relations with the Warsaw Pact countries. The conclusion was that the stakes remained high and Bonn's negotiations should be cautiously accelerated. But in view of the East Berlin position, attempts to improve relations with the GDR should be temporarily shelved. Thus, for the first time, a separate *Deutschlandpolitik* was dissected from the larger *Ostpolitik*; the former being side stepped and the latter intensified. Paradoxically, by it's own actions East Berlin was becoming increasingly isolated from both Eastern and Western Europe, a long-standing FRG goal.

The GDR also initiated a thorough policy review in the wake of the Kassel meeting. East Berlin was in danger not only of isolation but of being ostracized by its allies for acting as an obstruction to the achievement of their own respective interests vis-à-vis the FRG. The GDR was becoming the Soviets' principal opponent in the Pact's councils, assuming Rumania's former role as a focal point of dissent. Indeed it now appears that one reason for the decision to abandon the Pact's customary preference for multilateral bargaining between East and West in favor of bilateral negotiations was to appease Rumania and at the same time reduce East German interference. East Berlin had sought to amplify its self-appointed role as the monitor and guardian of the Pact's German policy. This had required a progressively more assertive foreign policy against both the West and its allies. But as the polemical threat from West Germany declined, East Berlin's leverage against its partners also diminished. The perils of intransigence were gradually compounded by the growing indifference of its allies.

East German estrangement became increasingly apparent in the treaties signed in Moscow in August and in Warsaw in November. The Soviets agreed to drop the provisions of the first draft treaty that explicitly related to East Germany and reinforced Allied rights in Berlin. Warsaw stated informally that it would establish diplomatic relations with Bonn when its treaty was ratified. Furthermore, at the Pact meeting convened on December 2, 1970 to consider formally the two treaties with Bonn and the latest Western détente proposals regarding European security, it became even more clear that the GDR's allies were willing to reach compromise with the FRG rather than defend East Berlin's maximum interests. The communiqué dropped the customary charges against West Germany and called for the pursuit of détente rather than confrontation. For the first time, it did not oppose Bonn's formula of two states in one nation and omitted demands for East German recognition as a precondition for further moves towards détente. Finally the communiqué paid tribute to the Soviet and Polish treaties as major contributions to peaceful coexistence, an implied slight to East Berlin for failing to follow suit. East Germany was in danger of weakening its influence within the Pact without advancing its individual interests. The meeting of the Pact nations in December confirmed that a new position on German policy had been decided upon and that the GDR was a singular but cautious opponent. The other six members now endorsed the two-Germanys policy and East Berlin now would have to rely increasingly on its own resources to reach an accommodation with Bonn.

Ulbricht was sensitive to the pitfalls in the changing situation, and, in speeches made during the summer of 1970, he gradually dropped his former maximalist demands. After the signing of the Soviet-West German Treaty, he called for normalization of relations between the GDR and the Federal Republic on the basis only of equality.[91] After the December meeting, he reported to the 14th SED Central Committee Plenum that a change had been made in the Pact's German policy and called for a solution of the Berlin question based on merely a reduction of the Federal Republic's presence in West Berlin, not on Bonn's recognition of its status as an independent political entity.[92] Some movement was becoming visible in the East German stance, although the party Plenum insisted again on the necessity of recognition.

On the West German side, the recognition issue became the center of a new phase of public debate. During the 1969 election campaign the question focused mainly on the legal aspects, the political problem of the viability of the East German state, and the implications of recognition for its legitimacy. But in January 1970 the SPD's Deputy Leader Herbert Wehner pointed out that recognition of the GDR "would be too little."[93] The issue was no longer recognition or nonrecognition or whether contractual agreements could be concluded with the GDR. Legal accords were less important than the political conditions for mutual accommodation. Coexistence was not enough! A degree of settlement was required that would relieve the respective grievances of the two Germanys but would not obviate their joint claims to a more permanent arrangement.

The complexity of the issue was further demonstrated during the lengthy litigation in the West German Supreme Court when the CSU challenged the legality of the *Ostverträge*. For example, the CSU argued that the Federal Republic could not make a case for recognizing the GDR under West German public law and that recognition under international law presupposes that both parties regard each other as foreign states. Nonrecognition need not be equated with an assumption of nonexistence, but recognition would virtually negate four-power responsibility for all Germany and undermine West Berlin's legal basis and security. Furthermore, there was a grave danger that recognition would reinforce Germany's partition. After gaining diplomatic credibility, the GDR could reduce other ties with the FRG without impairing its interests in preserving the division. In other words, the partition would be a political, not a constitutional, matter, and recognition of the GDR as a fully

sovereign state would seriously reduce Bonn's ability to ameliorate the effects of the division. Finally, there is little concrete
evidence that the Soviets would be prepared to accept the
consequent reduction in their authority on German matters
inherent in full recognition and the accompanying erosion of
four-power responsibilities.[94] The logic of these arguments has
led to the conclusion that full legal recognition of the GDR is
incompatible with existing political realities and that the correct approach to inner-German relations should be to improve
political accommodation to the point that recognition would
become a nonissue.

With the failure of the German summit meetings and the
relegation of *Deutschlandpolitik* to the background, however,
the prospects for a political accommodation were lessened and
were only gradually transferred to the new venue of the Berlin
question. From the outset of the Soviet-West German reconciliation in 1968 and 1969, Bonn had insisted that settlement of the
Berlin issue had to be a basic ingredient in the final package
representing FRG legal adjustments with Pact countries. The
Western allies concurred by mounting pressure against the
USSR to participate in the Four-Power talks on the future of
Berlin. After agreement was reached to conduct the Soviet and
Polish talks, Moscow reluctantly concurred, on February 10,
1970, to attend Four-Power discussions on Berlin, which
opened on March 26. This was the first time since 1959 that the
Four Powers had met over the Berlin question and the first time
since the postwar era that they had met on this issue without
Soviet pressure. During the first seven sessions, however, an
impasse developed as a result of the presentation of traditional,
well-known positions. To dislodge the discussions, Bonn rein-
troduced the tactic of *junktim,* first applied to link West German participation in the European security conference with
East German adjustment on political questions. In July,
Foreign Minister Walter Scheel argued that the Soviet Union
could not logically conclude an agreement with the Federal
Republic while it was pursuing a deliberate policy of tension
over the Berlin issue.[95] Later Brandt firmly coupled West German ratification of the Polish and Soviet treaties with a Berlin

accord.[96] As the talks progressed, it was agreed that implementation of a final agreement would require concurrence of both Germanys, necessitating reopening the inner-German talks.

During the fall of 1970, a series of events worsened relations between the super powers and delayed the Berlin talks even more. Soviet harrassment of autobahn traffic, violations of the cease fire along the Suez Canal, and attempts to construct a shore-supply base for nuclear submarines at Cienfuegos, Cuba, were viewed in Washington as being incompatible with détente. Gromyko met with Nixon in October and an informal accord was reached that provided the basis for continuing the Berlin talks. Gromyko then visited the two Germanys and both agreed to resume their dialogue. At Bonn's insistence it was to be conducted at the ministerial, not the summit level. But at the first and second meetings on November 27 and December 23, a stalemate soon emerged. Michael Kohl, East Berlin's chief negotiator, from the GDR wanted to focus the discussion on the West Berlin's status and access rights, which Egon Bahr had been instructed should remain under the exclusive purview of the four Allied powers. Bahr sought to steer the talks toward general East-West German problems. Little was achieved and the talks were temporarily suspended while attention was shifted to the conclusion of the *Ostpolitik* phase before seeking settlement of the Berlin question.

East-West German talks proved to be the least productive contacts at that time of all East-West exchanges. They were disappointing to the FRG, alarming to the GDR, and frustrating to the Four Powers. The reasons for the lack of progress were the lingering doctrinaire and ideological elements in the positions of both sides, the obduracy of Ulbricht himself, the imprecision in the FRG's long-term objectives and immediate aims, and the inability up to that time of the Four Powers to determine clearly their role in the settlement process. The latter reason was probably the most significant. No negotiations of major East-West German problems could begin before the Four Powers determined those all-German issues over which they would reserve authority and what problems and authority would be relegated to the two Germanys. The crux of reserved Four-Power authority was Berlin. Until the issues of its status and accessibility were resolved, the other obstacles appeared to be disproportionately large. By the time the Four-Power disputes were refined, however, these obstacles were also diminished or eliminated.

THE ROLE OF BERLIN IN THE INNER-GERMAN TALKS

The breakdown of the Bahr-Kohl talks pointed out that differences between the two Germanys went beyond the issue of recognition. The more basic problem was that it was unclear at that juncture whether the two Germanys could deal with each other over Berlin or larger German questions without specifically delegated authorization to do so by the Four Powers. Since the Four Powers reserved for themselves original rights of sovereignty over Germany until a peace treaty restored those rights to designated German authorities, no subordinate entity could legally arrogate to itself either a portion or all of those rights. The Preamble and Part I of the Potsdam Agreement defined those rights broadly as the authority to insure that Germany would never again disturb international peace. The original occupation documents were unilaterally violated by both sides, such as the rearming of both Germanys, without theoretically negating the legality of the surviving portions of the accords. Indeed unilateral actions by one power regarded as violations by others were subject to contest again without complete abrogation of the original prerogatives. For example, the Western powers challenged the Soviets' incorporation of East Berlin into the GDR and the final Berlin Protocol referred to no specific sectors, but to the greater Berlin area, that is, the perimeters of the four occupation sectors. Until the Four Powers themselves could reach agreement on the scope of their authority in Berlin, it was difficult to issue a specific mandate to the two Germanys to conduct talks. Accordingly, the East-West German discussions were suspended until the Four-

Power Protocol was concluded.[97] In the interval tensions remained unabated.[98]

The Four Powers were in general agreement on their determination to preserve the special status of Berlin. The Western Allies had suspended Articles 23 and 144(2) of the West German Basic Law (constitution) of 1949 on the grounds that Berlin was not a *Land* (province) but a special entity within the Federal Republic. The focal point of nearly two years of negotiating between 1970 and 1971 was the precise nature and scope of this special status that centered on four main issues. The contending positions can be briefly summarized:

Zugang or access rights. The Allies claimed that the transportation of civilian goods and persons between West Berlin and the Federal Republic should proceed without hindrance and should be subject merely to routine customs checks. The Soviets countered that, based on its international treaty with the GDR, East Berlin now had complete responsibility for access across its sovereign territory, except for military traffic, which should be recognized by the Western powers.

Zutritt or travel to East Berlin and the GDR. The Allies wanted the Four Powers to direct that arrangements be made between the West Berlin Senate and the GDR for West Berliners to visit East Berlin and the GDR on the same basis as other citizens of the Federal Republic. The Soviets maintained that there was neither cause nor legal grounds for such a directive since West Berliners resided in an independent political entity and were not citizens of the FRG.

Zuordnung or West Berlin's political status. The Allies insisted on Soviet recognition of the existing realities in the ties between West Berlin and the FRG; they were unprepared to accept any substantive change in the city's status. The Soviets maintained that, as an independent political entity, the exercise of the Federal Government's presence in West Berlin was a provocation and must be suspended. Furthermore, the Soviets had recognized East Berlin as the capital of the GDR and therefore relegated Four-Power authority exclusively to West Berlin. Thus, they insisted that the USSR shared equal authority with the Allies in West Berlin.

Vertretung or diplomatic representation. The Allies held that West Berlin and its population remained under the legal purview of the federal Government and that Bonn should represent their interests abroad, both as individuals and in a collective sense. The Soviets claimed that, as an independent political entity, West Berlin must represent itself abroad.

These positions were far apart. The issues were more complex and more important to the national interests of the main parties than the earlier agreements between Bonn and Pact members. Within these differences priorities varied, with the Allies placing greatest emphasis on guaranteed civilian access and the Soviets on the status of West Berlin.

Over two decades of Soviet and East German pressure had changed the nature of West Berlin. The city's political character had been altered by the East's strategy of forcing it to "wither on the vine." The population had become physically older and the students the most radical in West Germany. The professional and middle-class businessmen had moved in increasing numbers to the "mainland," despite heavy annual FRG subsidies for West Berlin industrial undertakings.[99]

The Soviets' attempted strategy of withering West Berlin on the vine was designed to capitalize on the city's exposed position by seeking to reduce the psychological linkage between West Berlin and the FRG without increasing the burden of these bonds, for excessive dependency might resurrect the emotional ties of earlier Berlin crises. Lowering the Federal appearance would both reduce the physical ties with Bonn and diminish the symbolic position of West Berlin as the West's beleaguered outpost, thereby undermining its visibility. At the same time, the Soviets tried to insure the durability of their role in future West Berlin matters to maintain effective influence over both Germanys.

Bonn gradually recognized that there was no flexibility on the Soviet side on the issue of the presence of the Federal Government. After nearly a year of Four-Power talks, the federal minister for inner-German relations, Egon Franke, publicly outlined a compromise formula, whereby the presence of Federal offices and agencies would remain in the city and

Federal officials would continue routine visits but would refrain from performing official activities, such as conducting presidential elections or signing legislated statutes.[100] In exchange, the Soviets would have to recognize the existing cultural, economic, and political ties between the city and West Germany. Demonstrations of Federal bonds had been made explicitly to underscore the unity of the city with the Republic, but they could be reduced or dropped if adequate guarantees were provided of respect for the existing status of the city.

The shift in the FRG attitude on Federal activities in West Berlin plus its firm stand on *junktim* produced movement toward settlement. The Soviets leaked the confidential copy of their working paper for the Four-Power meeting of March 26.[101] It was later confirmed as authentic. The Soviet paper gave ground on the transit problem, agreeing to the transportation of sealed vehicles based upon validated documents (accepting the Allied position), and on ties between the city and the FRG, while holding firm on the city's special status and the Soviet role in the preservation of that position. Concessions were now made in rapid order by both sides.[102]

Walter Ulbricht's continuing obstinate resistance against the Soviet concessions led to his replacement in May as party leader by Erich Honecker. The change in the Soviet position on a wide variety of East-West problems became apparent soon afterwards. The impasse in the SALT I talks was broken by the decision to limit discussions to antiballistic missile defenses. On May 14, Brezhnev announced that the USSR was prepared to explore with NATO countries the prospects for mutual troop reductions.[103] Honecker and Stoph met with Brezhnev in Moscow and issued a communiqué stating that an agreement on Berlin would serve the interests of all interested parties.[104] Finally, in his speech to the Eighth SED Party Congress Honecker dropped references to West Berlin as an independent political entity and cited only its "special political status," but he insisted that the city had never been a part of the FRG, attacking the problem from a different angle. Yet, he omitted the traditional demand that legal recognition of the GDR was the precondition for the conclusion of a Berlin accord.[105] On September 3, 1971 the foreign ministers of the Four Powers signed the Quadripartite Agreement that was to be supplemented by enabling treaties negotiated between the appropriate German authorities. The final package, known as the Berlin Protocol, was signed on June 3, 1972.[106]

The documents within the protocol represent compromises, omissions, and provisions subject to differing interpretations. On the status of Berlin, the Four Powers agreed to disagree. The Soviets dropped their demand that East Berlin be cited as the capital of the GDR and the Allies conceded that the major issues pertained chiefly to the Western sectors. Since no consensus was reached on the definition of Greater Berlin or the Four Powers' authority they remained legally as stated in the Potsdam Agreement.

On the relationship between West Berlin and the Federal Republic, Part II, paragraph B, reiterated the Western position and Annex II contained a formal note from the three Allies to the Soviets defining their positions: ". . . in the exercise of their rights and responsibilities" the ties between the Western sectors of Berlin and the Federal Republic will be *"maintained and developed,"* but the city would continue not to be a *constituent part of the FRG,* nor governed by it. In other words, its special status would continue as it had developed since 1949. But the protocol also provides that "the situation which has developed in the area [apparently meaning greater Berlin] . . . shall not be changed unilaterally." Such wording may have been a Western attempt to underscore Four-Power responsibilities for East Berlin if the Soviets should become assertive about their rights in the Western Sectors. As Secretary of State William Rogers said at the signing ceremonies, the protocol expressly states that the Four Powers concluded the accord without prejudice to their legal positions and that their individual and joint rights and responsibilities remain unchanged.[107] Yet, when Bonn decided under the authorization to "develop ties" by establishing the Federal Environmental Agency and a training school for the Common Market in West

Berlin, the East Germans interpreted these moves as unilateral actions that affected the city's status and ties. After a series of protests, they retaliated by harrassing autobahn traffic.

In a separate note to the FRG, the three Allies defined the changes in the Federal demonstrative presence. No serious alterations of substantive relations were expected. *Bundestag* committees would continue to meet in the city and conduct routine business, but no plenary sessions of the *Bundestag* and *Bundesrat* would be permitted. The chancellor and president were precluded from conducting acts in the city which would imply the exercise of direct authority over the Western sectors. The Federal government was to be represented in West Berlin by a permanent liaison office, and Federal workers were to remain at their posts (in 1973 there were 24,000 Federal employees in West Berlin compared to 22,000 in Bonn). The FRG has complied with these constraints.

The Soviet presence in West Berlin remains the subject of controversy. The Soviets continue to participate in the joint administration of the Spandau prison in the British Sector and in the Berlin Air Safety Center in the American Sector, and they maintain a Soviet war memorial in the British Sector. The agreement provided for the establishment of a Consulate General and several commercial enterprises in the Western sectors. But Agreed Minute II imposed precise limits on the number of Soviet personnel that could be assigned to these organizations: 20 to the Consulate, 20 to the Soviet Foreign Trade Association, one in each warehouse, six in the Intourist office, and five in the Aeroflot office. This is a severe limitation designed to minimize both the Soviet operations and political profile.

The Consulate General is accredited to the three Allied military governments and is prohibited from engaging in political activities or functions related to quadripartite rights and responsibilities. Egon Bahr argued that Soviet agreement to such a tightly restricted presence had positive features for the West. Accreditation to the three Allies would demonstrate that the Soviets had no original rights in West Berlin. It was a foreign power and only the Allies exercised sovereignty over West Berlin. These exclusive rights could not be jeopardized by

West Berlin's ties with the FRG because the Allies had legally delegated authority for such relations to the two entities. For Bahr the Soviet presence would serve as a serious legal and physical constraint against Moscow.[108]

But the Soviets and East Germans apparently agreed to these provisions for different reasons. Bahr conceded that the maneuver enhanced West Berlin's special status as the "third phenomenon." The Soviets, however, concluded that the terms for their new presence gave them similar advantages to those the Allies would enjoy when they established embassies in East Berlin. Indeed, the Consulate might later be interpreted as a surrogate demonstration of West Berlin's political independence. Since 1972 the Soviets have maintained an unobtrusive image, but they also have made repeated references to West Berlin's independent status. (Only two days after the signing of the protocol, both Gromyko and Honecker stated that in reality it was a "quadripartite agreement on West Berlin.")[109]

Annex IV of the agreement registers the Soviets' acceptance of Bonn's right to represent West Berlin abroad. The Federal Government may provide consular services for permanent residents abroad, conclude agreements and treaties with other states that are applicable in West Berlin, represent West Berlin's interests in international conferences and organizations, and continue to issue passports and personal identification cards to West Berlin citizens.

The issue focuses on the nature of the ties between the FRG and West Berlin and their legal implications. The West Germans use the words *Band* or *Bindung,* which have a broad, yet durable connotation. The wording in the Russian texts is far more restrictive and technical. The Soviets insist that there is no basis for any legal connections between the two, and therefore Bonn can only represent the political and commercial *interests* of West Berlin. It can provide no legal aid or assistance to an individual in or from West Berlin. This prohibition stems from the Western sectors' special status and the lack of definitive citizenship for its inhabitants. The *Ostverträge* and the *Grundvertrag* omitted provisions for the legal citizenship for the inhabitants of either East Germany or West Berlin. The West German Supreme Court ruled that the treaties made no changes in the existing FRG citizenship laws, a strict interpretation that precludes a solution such as dual citizenship. Thus, in the Soviets' view, such acts as issuing passports are administrative functions and are devoid of any legal ramifications.[110]

The problem of citizenship and legal rights remains open, subject to unilateral legal and political decisions or negotiations. In 1975 Moscow and Bonn opened consideration of a compromise whereby, in cases involving West Berliners in Eastern Europe, the respective court in West Berlin would request assistance (that is, documents or testimony) from the appropriate authority in Eastern Europe, without submitting legal queries through national political channels.

The Soviets have sound legal grounds and strong political incentives to maintain their position. The Western sectors under the protocol are not a constituent part of the FRG and, therefore, not subject to its legal processes. Moreover, the reinforcement of these legal barriers strengthens the arguments for Berlin's autonomous status. Finally, the authorization for West Berlin courts to act individually on behalf of litigants weakens Bonn's stand of the quality of its ties with the sectors.[111]

Egon Bahr has been credited in April 1971 with separating the political and legal issues from the pragmatic problems of reducing the personal hardships of inhabitants of both East and West Berlin. The Four Powers had individual and joint rights and responsibilities and their respective interpretations of them, but this should not impede agreement on "nonpolitical," humanitarian questions of guaranteed access, the settlement of intracity problems, and strengthening the provision of legal protection under the Basic Law for West Berliners. The principle of *Zutritt*, entry of West Berliners to East Berlin and the GDR, lay at the heart of humanizing the partition. Part II paragraph C and annex III of the protocol provided that the USSR would assure West Berliners entry through the Wall for personal reasons or as tourists on the same basis as other visitors, subject to normal customs procedures. The details of these provisions were to be negotiated by the West Berlin *Senat* and the GDR. On December 20, 1971 an agreement on the "Facilitation and Improvement of Travel and Visitors' Traffic" was signed in East Berlin.[112]

East Berlin at the time was and remains hypersensitive about its vulnerability to Western influence. Accordingly, it has sought to limit the exposure of its residents to West Berliners. It imposed a ceiling of 30 days of visits per year for each resident of the Western sectors, which could be extended in hardship cases. But they were not granted equal status with other visitors. Instead of a visa, which would have implied recognition, the West Berliners were granted an "entry permit." Criminals and refugees who fled after August 1961 were denied access. The accord also provides for the appointment of mediators to resolve disputes about its implementation. If they remained unresolved, the misunderstandings were to be referred to the GDR government and the West Berlin *Senat*. From the West Berliners' viewpoint, the accord was a delicate balance between controlled access to East Berlin and recognition of West Berlin's status, which nonetheless created a significant hard-currency income for the GDR and provided a channel for consumer goods.[113]

From the West's perspective, the problems associated with access of civilian transportation between West Berlin and the FRG was the most important aspect of improving the personal conditions for the West Berliners.[114] In part II paragraph A and annex I of the protocol, the USSR agreed that the transit of civilian persons and goods would be handled in the most simple and expeditious manner—indeed, it was to receive preferential treatment. Customs controls of persons transiting GDR territory were to be limited to identification checks and routine inspections. The annex also defined the conditions for claiming misuse of accessways under which *the GDR* could deny passage or search travelers. The FRG was to pay a lump sum of 234.9 million DM during the years 1972 and 1975 for tolls and maintenance costs. The accord specified the details for handling goods in sealed containers. Finally, a comission of East and West Germans was established to resolve disputes.[115]

The significance of the access accord is that the USSR agreed to accept responsibility for guaranteeing transit of civilian persons and goods. It had consistently maintained earlier that the sovereign rights over the access routes had been transferred in 1955 to the GDR. (Military transit is controlled exclusively by the Four Powers.) If fully applied, this would undercut the GDR claims to complete sovereignty. But the clause authorizing East Berlin, not Moscow, to determine when misuse or violations had occurred was an open-ended permit to resort to harrassment tactics whenever the occasion warranted. Thus the Soviets' seeming recantation on the sovereignty issue has little genuine validity; surface transit conditions have improved but their guarantee remains questionable.

After repeated threats that the defections violated the access provisions in the Quadripartite Agreement, the GDR temporarily imposed rigid inspection controls on January 26, 1974. In the two years after signing the protocol, 215 persons were arrested by GDR authorities for misusing the access routes and received increasingly stiffer sentences.[118] Despite the continued possibility of harrassment, there was a 60 percent rise over the previous three-year period (see below).[116]

Clarification of the status of West Berlin and its legal and political relationships was one of the most difficult aspects of all East-West negotiations relating to the German issue. The Four-Power protocol contributed significantly to the more precise definition of contested issues, appropriate jurisdictions, and ultimate responsibilities. Reducing ambiguities advanced the normalization process, primarily on functional and technical matters. But West Berlin's status continues to be essentially a political problem and the focus of contending political interests and rival interpretations on legal positions. As long as the two Germanys remain "limited adversaries," West Berlin will persist as a competitive source of leverage for both states. It will also function as a primary basis of Four-Power influence in the on-going controversy over the German problem. A central feature of the protocol was the provision of a

negotiating framework for the two Germanys that would hope-
fully further advance the normalization of their relations and,
thereby, reduce the remaining conflictual aspects of West Berlin's situation. This framework, however, remains to be fully
utilized.

The statistics cited in the next chapter indicate both the early
euphoria and the constraints accompanying the protocol; an
atmosphere that gradually changed into greater sobriety and
realism as the *Grundvertrag* negotiations reached completion.
Yet, the status and stature of West Berlin itself gradually began
to stabilize. Despite many lean years, West Berlin remains
West Germany's largest industrial city, with an annual industrial production worth $10 billion and a gross income of $20
billion. Yet during the East German retrenchment period between 1969 and 1972, it lost nearly one quarter of its industrial
jobs, and investment activity declined. But the economic slide
has now been reversed, and West Berlin has developed long-
range plans to generate 825,000 jobs in a city of 1.5 million by
1990. In the short term, the present bürgermeister, Dietrich
Stobbe, is actively seeking new investments. Some loans and
investments can be obtained at 3.5 percent interest from funds
still available under the Marshall Plan. West Berlin itself provides tax incentives and the FRG allows 30 percent income tax
reductions for companies and individuals, a waiver of the 13
percent value-added-tax, and a 25 percent grant on new equipment purchases.

One phase of the plan is the expansion of the three main
traditional Berlin industries: electronics, machinery and heavy
equipment (including turbines and locomotives), and metal-
working. Next, West Berlin hopes to expand the potential of its
nearly 200 research and development firms, which, in turn
should attract small and medium-sized firms that are capable of
rapid innovation. Finally, West Berlin is seeking a major bid for
the convention market. A $300 million International Congress
complex already has bookings for two years after its completion in 1979. Accompanying hotel construction will provide
3000 additional beds.[117]

The accomplishment of these ambitious plans hinges on the

prevailing political climate and mutual compliance with both the letter and spirit of the Berlin Protocol. The relative success of these plans is also likely to serve to indicate how effectively the *Grundvertrag* and other East-West German agreements will be applied in the future.

Chapter IV

Scope and Nature of Inner-German Relations

THE GRUNDVERTRAG: THE CLIMAX OF THE SPD's OPENING TO THE EAST

Probably the most important aspect of Four-Power Berlin negotiations was the development of a formula for stabilizing relations between the Germanys and of a framework for cooperation. The Four Powers directed that the two sides negotiate a treaty dealing with the technical aspects of traffic and transportation between the states (separate from the Berlin access accord).[118] As a concession to the GDR's demand for recognition, Bonn finally agreed that the accord would be in the form of a treaty and would be afforded the appropriate legal authority in international law.[119] The FRG-GDR Traffic and Transportation Agreement was signed in April, 1972 and dealt primarily with functional problems. Its political utility was that it afforded sufficient confidence for both sides to encourage negotiations on the Basic Treaty (*Grundvertrag*).

The Basic Treaty was the product of a sensitive timetable that generated pressure on both sides. Because of the *junktim* linkage between ratification of the Moscow and Warsaw treaties with the conclusion of the Berlin Protocol, the supplementary agreements between West Berlin and the GDR had to be reached by the end of 1971. The FRG-GDR Traffic and Transportation Accord was needed by early 1972 to counter the CDU's argument that before an imminent election campaign the *Ostverträge* impaired German interests without reducing the partition. The ratification debate was scheduled for May and the *Ostverträge* were barely passed (because three CDU deputees defected). But the erosion of the coalition's majority to an even 50 percent forced Brandt to seek a national election, set for November 19. In the interim he sought agreement on a general treaty with the GDR as the capstone of his *Ostpolitik* that could focus the election on the success of SPD foreign policy.[120] The *Grundvertrag* was signed in December 1972 and came into force on June 12, 1973 and was judged valid in July by the West German Constitutional Court.

The treaty dealt with several central concepts of international law, including the renunciation of force in terms almost identical to those in the other *Ostverträge,* border regulations and the mutual recognition of inviolability (inherent in the renunciation of force concept), and a guarantee that ths treaty would not interfere with previous agreements.[121] In accompanying letters. Bonn insisted that, while borders should not be physically violated, they must remain subject to change, and even abrogation, based upon inner-German agreement or an overall European settlement (the so-called European clause which was also incorporated in the Helsinki Final Act of the Conference on Security and Cooperation in Europe).

Bonn also insisted on minimal structural improvements that would facilitate inner-German relations, conditioned, of course, on the overall climate of détente. The German question was explicitly kept open, by acknowledging disagreement about reunification and reaffirming Allied responsibility for a German settlement, preferably within the framework of a European peace treaty. Both parties recognized that the treaty was only an important step in advancing first détente, then normalcy, and at some future time possibly a form of unity. To this end Bonn pledged to seek speedy Western recognition of East Berlin and its admission into international organizations.

But the treaty and its supporting documents included ambiguities that led to varying interpretations.[122] The clause extending its provisions to West Berlin was qualified in that it would be "decided in each case arising," and was not binding on future agreements. The GDR agreed to accept the exchange of permanent representatives rather than ambassadors. In an accompanying letter, Bonn declared that this formula demonstrated that an equal position of the Democratic Republic in the international arena meant no weakening of our concept by which the West German state was not a foreign country. Yet the letter recognized the GDR as an independent state with responsibilities for its own affairs at home and abroad. In the treaty preamble, however, both parties agreed to disagree about the basic question of the nation's existence.

Bonn had quietly shelved its demands for reunification based on self-determination and the establishment of common institutions, but insisted upon preserving the hope for all Germans of achieving a less exact form of reunification after Europe's division became more malleable.[123] Yet, for East Berlin, partition remained the indispensable foundation of its legitimacy. German reunification was one of the main points considered by the Federal Constitutional Court in its interpretation of July 1973 of the treaty's legality. The overriding view was that all agreements with the GDR must comply with the FRG Basic Law which cited reunification as a national objective. Yet, the interpretation left room for bargaining maneuver and tended to reinforce the government's emphasis on normalization.

Thus the treaty is a hastily concluded accord with fundamental contradictions. It is not a definitive statement of the nature of inner-German relations, although it includes several specific principles of international law that prescribe the minimum conditions for cooperation. The treaty is primarily a mutually agreed framework for further political negotiations as required by the normalization process.

LEVELS OF COOPERATION AND CONTINUING DISPUTE

Peter C. Ludz has characterized the relationship between the two Germanys after the treaty came in force as constituting both cooperation and demarcation.[124] A survey first of the cooperative ventures that have been concluded or are being negotiated covers a wide variety of issues. Several structural additions have been created to facilitate contacts. Federal Undersecretary of State, Günther Gaus, has been accredited to the East German Foreign Ministry as Bonn's Plenipotentiary in East Berlin, and the GDR's representative, Michael Kohl, has presented his credentials to the Chancellory (an important distinction since he is accredited to the encumbent Chancellor not to the Federal President). A second channel was established by accrediting GDR Deputy Foreign Minister, Kurt Nier, to the FRG mission in East Berlin.

The primary East-West German agreements have also established several new institutional structures intended to facilitate the resolution of inner-German problems in specific areas. The Border Commission was set up in accordance with the Supplementary Protocol to the *Grundvertrag,* as well as the Explanatory Statement to the Protocol on the Functions of the Commission agreed to by both sides. The commission is charged with the responsibility for confirming and marking the border line between the two Germanys, based on the 1954 London Agreement and later Allied accords. It is also responsible for the resolution of problems arising from the nature and definition of the border itself. Much of the work of the commission has been predetermined by earlier agreements and has been largely accomplished along the 1346 km border. Thus uncertainties have been avoided and the possibility of incidents limited along the boundary. The commission has held over 50 sessions between January 31, 1973 and June 1979; it is now primarily concerned with the problems and mutual recognition of the responsibilities for maintaining the waterways and their shores along the common border (see below). In a comprehensive document, the November 1978 Protocol on the Principles and Activities of the Border Commission recognized the principle of continuous border identification and demarcation, and compiled the 26 relevant previous accords.[125]

Both sides recognized the mutual interest in taking joint actions along the frontier that would establish a continuously precise definition (necessary in cases of rivers and erosion), control of damages along either side, regulate contagious diseases, facilitate joint use of dam waters, insure cross-border water supplies, delineate fishing rights, assure recreational privileges, provide for exploitation of transborder resources, such as mines, and provide for mutual assistance in the event of natural calamity affecting the boundary. Thus the November 1978 Protocol represents the culmination of years of negotiation and indicates areas of on-going activities.

The second organization, the Transit and Transportation Commission, was established to resolve problems resulting from the differences of opinion and interpretation of the agreement and to improve traffic and transportation conditions. Through the commission the two sides agreed in December 1975 to undertake the basic reconstruction of the Helmstedt-Berlin autobahn and to open the Staaken border crossing point. These were the first transit and rail improvements, followed by the December 1977 arrangement to expand the Helmstedt/Marienborn autobahn to six lanes. The commission also deals with a variety of specific problems, such as, the right established in the *Grundvertrag* of West Germans and West Berliners to travel to any part of the GDR, free choice of border exit points, permission to visit friends not just relatives, repeated visits per year, tourism and tourist excursions, regulation for the use of private vehicles, opening of new highway border crossings and traffic regulations within border areas—including day excursions (about 480,000 visitors in 1978).

Specifically, the Transit and Transportation Commission participated in the negotiations of the November 1978 Announcement by the Federal Government on the Results of the Negotiations with the GDR on Traffic Questions and Settlements Regulations.[126] This comprehensive package included measures for the improvement of traffic conditions into West Berlin, Bonn's agreement to pay 1.2 billion DM over four years for the construction of the Berlin-Hamburg autobahn, the FRG's acceptance of sharing expenses of 120 million DM for improved transit waterways to Berlin, payment by Bonn of 70 million DM for the repair and belated reopening of the Teltow Canal, Bonn's lump-sum annual payment of 525 million DM between 1980 and 1989 for transit costs to and from West Berlin, and the creation of the funds for noncommercial monetary transfers.

Despite these significant contributions to improved cooperation, the commissions remain primarily functional structures that can be convened at the request of either side, and thereby represent an institutional connection that is probably as important per se as the significance of their efforts to strengthen relations. While the results have been less than were initially expected, this does not minimize the interest of both sides in perpetuating their continued existence. The East Germans view the permanence of the commissions as a reinforcing mechanism for their claims to legitimacy and separate statehood. The West Germans accept the commissions as appropriate organs for the settlement of functional problems, a mechanism for shunting small problems to small agencies that helps focus more important issues into the more conventional intergovernmental channels, where they can be more effectively controlled and linked to other issues.

There are several additional forums that are utilized with varying frequency and success. The Clearing Office for Inter-Zonal Trade (*Treuhandstelle für den Interzonenhandel*) was originally established in the August 1951 Berlin Accord, which was re-negotiated in 1960 and 1969. Representatives meet every two weeks to discuss inner-German trade and payment issues. Additionally, two working groups have been established to discuss the expanding number of mutual legal problems. A committee on public health was established in 1974 and held five meetings within three years. Negotiations between the two sides are conducted in other issue areas as required by designated ministerial representation without formal committee structures.

Bilateral negotiations stimulated by the 1972 agreements reflect the sporadic relations between the political entities since 1949 and are probably more important than the structural changes themselves. Between 1949 and 1978, 73 formal joint interstate agreements have been signed. (Annex A contains a complete list.) The categories listed in Table I range from accords on railway transportation to Wall passes, to traffic insurance, to trade.

It should be noted that the table does not reflect the relative

TABLE I[127]

Categorization of FRG–GDR Agreements, 1949–1979

West Berlin travel and facilities	10
Border issues including Berlin and mining disputes	13
Trade, credits, and money transfers	9
Shipping	7
Travel FRG–GDR	8
Transportation (rail)	6
Wall passes (Berlin)	6
Post and telecommunications	5
Traffic problems and insurance	4
Sports	2
Miscellaneous	3
Total	73

importance of any category or attempt to rank the priorities either side attached to any accord. Despite some overlap, it does indicate the areas of continuing concern of both parties and, by referring to Annex A, it reveals the continued frustrations, along with the partial resolutions.

A content analysis of the accords in Annex A is a fairly accurate barometer of the substantive nature of relations between three German entities. It shows that high-level talks between respective bureaucratic offices were opened as soon as the separate Germanys began to materialize, primarily on the functional aspects of transportation; the GDR also conducted bilateral talks to consolidate its position and to gain FRG recognition of its annexation of East Berlin and thereby acceptance of Berlin's division and the separate status of the Western half (Item 7).

After 1967 the GDR changed priorities. Negotiations with Bonn became less critical in its consolidation and recognition process. This was probably due to the defensive nature of GDR policy after Rumania's opening to Bonn. The marginality of direct talks between 1967 and 1971 was probably also due to the growing obduracy of Ulbricht and GDR sensitivities about its vulnerability to West German diplomatic maneuvers. Wall passes were suspended, the 1954 travel accords were not renegotiated until 1973, and only a limited postal and telecommunication agreement was signed in April 1970. On the basis alone of the volume of agreements signed between 1967 and 1971, the period can be considered as the time when East Germany was retrenching. Thus, it is apparent that negotiating patterns reflected vagaries of political climates and mutual perceptions of risks and advantages to be gained by bargaining.

In 1971 five accords were signed, and for the first time Bonn agreed to use the word government, rather than ministry or bureau, indicating a debatable extension of *de jure* recognition to the GDR. In 1972 eight additional agreements were negotiated, including the most important, the transit accords and the *Grundvertrag*. Under the authority of these agreements, seven more were signed the following year (although four sets of incomplete negotiations were also initiated in 1973). A total of 16 were concluded in 1974 before a sharp decline to seven in 1975, five in 1976, only four in 1977, and four in 1978. It should be noted that many of the latter accords were merely annual extensions of previous agreements, such as tourist regulations and sports schedules. Others included mere trivia, such as an exchange of letters informing the FRG of minor construction undertakings. Of the total number of agreements, all but five were negotiated at the ministerial level.

The negotiations and agreements have contributed to improved cooperation in selected areas, but also to continued frustration and conflicting interests in others. In trade and economics, the agreements conclude by the Clearing Office for Inter-zoneal Trade resulted in the raising of FRG credits to

830 million VE (clearing units) annually and a tripling of inner-German trade from 1968 to 1977, when it stabilized. The Clearing Office concluded in 1976 an accord for the exploitation of soft coal deposits near Helmstedt-Harbke. Negotiations for the development of a natural gas field near Wustrow/Salzwedel were opened in 1975 but have not yet been concluded. The outstanding commercial questions remain largely outside the control of the FRG and GDR. These are problems of regional and worldwide economic recession and the difficulties of East Germany to introduce new technologies and products without extensive new credits, which West German bankers are increasingly reluctant to grant.

One of the areas of most extensive agreement has been in public health. The initial April 1974 accord, which included West Berlin because of medical not political reasons, entitles visitors of the respective other German state to gratuitous ambulance service and full hospitalization in the case of acute illness. The agreement provides for special treatment for contagious disease and regulates the exchange of information, prophylactic measures, and medication for treatment of contagious diseases. Exchange of information on drug abuse is authorized, as is data on trafficking. But exchanges on medical research and even techniques, have been restricted, mainly by Bonn which has relegated such issues to the category of science and technology, wherein related fields are involved. Representatives meet semiannually, and mainly routine matters of implementation are considered.

Sports is another area in which the two Germanys have agreed to disagree. The May 1974 protocol negotiated between the FRG *Deutscher Sportbund* and the GDR *Deutscher Turn- und Sportbund* established a schedule for the exchange of leading sportsmen. The schedule has been extended annually and, in some cases, the number of participants expanded. But the FRG's attempts to include a number of smaller provincial clubs has been blocked by the GDR's demand restricting competition to top athletes and clubs. Little progress is expected, despite Bonn's frequent reference to the CSCE Helsinki Final Act on this matter.

The issue of lump-sum payments for transit tolls for both private and commercial West German and West Berlin transit traffic has been a source of irritation for Bonn and pressure for East Berlin. Prior to the 1972 accords, the GDR periodically used transit tolls as a means of harrassment, either increasing the price or protracting payment procedures. Bonn accepted a lump-sum annual fixed settlement, but sought a reduction in price. East Berlin accepted the principle of making lump-sum payments, but increased the fee. It was finally agreed in the November 1978 Traffic Protocol, included in the announcement, that the FRG would pay 525 million annually from 1980 to 1985 as transit tolls between the FRG and West Berlin. This was one of the toughest negotiations with both sides feeling disadvantaged; East Berlin because of inflation and stagnation in trade, Bonn because of the potential economic vulnerability of West Berlin. This issue will likely remain one of the most contentious problems.

The initial agreement of April 1974 on noncommercial payments included settlements for pensions, social security, life insurarnce., alimony, personal claims, and personal bank claims. While no transfers were possible prior to 1974, some 30 million DM were transfered annually from the respective central banks. But far more payment requests were placed in the FRG than the GDR, and Bonn was forced in 1976 to refuse to accept further requests. Negotiations were concluded in the November 1978 announcement whereby the terms of the 1974 agreement were reaffirmed but the sum was increased from 30 million DM annually to 50 million DM to be held by the respective central banks from 1979 to 1982. East Berlin has strongly indicated that this represents a summary settlement period for all outstanding claims, but this is unrealistic from Bonn's viewpoint. It would deny the longevity of many claims and ignore those of Germans in Eastern Europe or emigrants from there.

There are other issues upon which negotiations have been conducted, but that have defied conclusion. One is the attempt to standardize traffic laws, which is complicated by dissimilarities in vehicle registration regulations, operator licensing ordinances, insurance company liability policies, insurance remuneration, penal codes, and litigation procedures. In this case long-standing practices are almost as divisive as the legal differences. Progress may be made on selected issues, but even small steps in this area are tied so closely to the unsolved juridical differences of the two systems that mutual agreement is unlikely. Indeed, the GDR may have concluded that this is an option best kept open should future traffic interference be required.

Likewise, serious talks on environmental problems have yet to be undertaken because of several practical questions including whether or not to consider West Berlin (the largest industrial city in either Germany); how the GDR can prevent West German industrial espionage, and what the costs of remedial actions might be. The talks also have been delayed because the socialist countries give environmental questions a low priority. After the FRG set up in 1974 the Federal Office of Environmental Control in West Berlin, the GDR has refused to reopen negotiations on pollution problems. Little progress is expected, therefore, except possibly in the borderlands and waterways where the FRG is particularly concerned with potassium sewage pollution.

The GDR has a higher interest than the FRG in scientific and technological exchanges. Bonn, however, has linked increased technological exchange with more genuine compliance with the Helsinki Final Act, requiring freer flow of information and people. Until the GDR agrees to include West Berlin in any agreements, little progress is expected.

Cultural exchanges are stymied over claims and counter claims for the possession of prewar art treasures. The FRG insists that present holdings were awarded legally by the Allies and are not subject to negotiations (the Allies have no interest in seeking a redistribution). The FRG is prepared to negotiate exchanges of artwork but not without adequate guarantees against confiscation. Negotiations are deadlocked on the issue, but both sides are seeking exchanges at a lower level under the auspices of local authorities. At present, the exchange of books, exhibitions, movies and television films, among other cultural attractions are negotiated on a "firm-to-firm" basis,

TABLE II[129]

Travel by West Germans to the GDR [a]

1967	1,423,738
1968	1,261,441
1969	1,107,077
1970	1,254,084
1971	1,267,355

Month	1972	1973	1974	1975	1976	1977 [b]
January	28,626	47,105	47,828	74,630	75,424	80,434
February	28,156	46,679	46,540	80,173	79,067	78,253
March	199,766	143,851	126,902	544,744	165,201	176,169
April	84,562	392,661	236,384	180,336	520,989	408,834
May	136,419	133,548	152,015	412,509	281,647	356,376
June	112,137	255,947	171,374	217,528	332,930	240,990

TABLE II (Continued)

Month	1972	1973	1974	1975	1976	1977 b
July	234,449	307,426	241,583	439,767	442,572	386,603
August	201,415	272,839	270,312	368,806	330,848	338,101
September	150,828	227,795	161,884	237,475	267,317	278,675
October	104,284	200,274	148,652	233,141	276,462	279,201
November	62,566	101,378	97,997	122,494	130,463	140,216
December	197,173	149,486	217,671	212,338	218,042	223,174
Total	1,540,381	2,278,989	1,919,141	3,123,941	3,120,962	2,987,026

a A West German is defined as a person, not necessarily a citizen, carrying FRG travel documents. These figures do not include an additional 13 percent of the 1976 total who travelled from third countries and an unspecified, but extensive, figure for air travel.

b These statistics were no longer publicly available for 1977. In 1978 and 1979 they include West Germans and foreigners.

without the protection of an overriding accord between the two states.

The legal problems between the Germanys have multiplied much faster than warranted by the mere implementation of the agreements, and have been magnified by the fundamentally different legal systems. They include the broader questions of citizenship, intercity or provincial relations between the centralized GDR and the federated FRG, "interoffice assistance" regarding personal claims of people who have fled the GDR, and conflicts between the civil law of the two Germanys. The *Grundvertrag* provides that legal assistance is to be made readily available. But progress on only an ad hoc basis can be expected at best.[128]

THE PRACTICAL UTILITIES OF THE EAST-WEST GERMAN ACCORDS

Many who have supported *Ostpolitik* in the past are now not so optimistic that pragmatic results can be expected from the concessions made in the *Ostverträge*. Yet many opponents have been genuinely surprised at the benefits, however varied, now enjoyed by West Germans and West Berliners compared to ten years ago. The statistics in the following tables ambivalently tend to support both perceptions.

There was a decline of 200,000 travelers during the retrenchment period between 1967 and 1971. A sharp increase was noted after the Traffic Treaty was signed and confidence increased in 1972. A marked drop was registered in 1974, undoubtedly due to the impact of East German autobahn harrassment, which was followed by an even faster rise in 1975. Travel between 1976 and 1978 appears to reflect the chill in inner-German relations and the deterioration in the various negotiations because it has levelled off at around three million. (This is still three times above the figure for the last 1960's.) The high initial growth rates were due primarily to family ties, then tourism and business, and finally to limited exchanges. The plateauing effect was due to a decline in tourism (only 120,000) and in inner-German relations, plus local irritations, such as currency regulations, that discouraged many travelers who had already visited the GDR. Yet about 1.4 million West Germans annually visit East Berlin and some 3.3 million visits are made by West Berliners to the East. Together with West Berliners 7.8 million traveled in 1978 to the GDR, a country of only 17 million. Finally, 100 million West Germans and West Berliners transited between the FRG and the city by all means of transportation between January 1972 and 1979.

These figures also reflect the political uncertainties and inconveniences that travelers suffered because of harassment during the retrenchment period; the number decreased to 440,000. Yet after 1972 travel increased to the point that, between 1967 and 1977 the figure nearly doubled. It is interesting to note that the decline in 1974 was only 57,000 compared to the 6.5 times greater drop in the number of West Germans who travelled to the GDR. This suggests that the West Berliners, for a variety of psychological, commercial, and political reasons, may be less intimidated by harassment tactics than are West Germans who indeed may have fewer incentives to visit Berlin or more readily use airlines. The ten-year growth rate for traffic to Berlin was only double compared to triple for the West Germans alone visiting the GDR, reinforcing the observation that the main West German incentive was familial relations and for West Berliners to break the isolation syndrome. This was reaffirmed by the 1977 surge of 1.6 million travelers, reportedly mainly West Berliners vacationing in the West.

Table IV is less complete than Tables I-III, which makes comparisons difficult. However, it is apparent that there was a 62 percent increase in 1972, followed by a relative constancy, a marked contrast to the tripling of West German traffic to the GDR. The comparison is made difficult, however, by the East German practice of including people who are expelled, legal emigrants, diplomats, business men, and persons acting in official capacities. It is clear that few scientists, much less tourists, receive exit visas for the FRG, which Bonn charged at the 1977 Belgrade Review Conference of CSCE was a flagrant violation of the Helsinki Final Act. (Yet in 1978 there were

TABLE III [a]

Travel by West Germans and West Berliners from the FRG by Land to West Berlin

Month	1967	1968	1969	1970	1971	1972
January	188,558	191,635	185,717	194,023	212,255	244,892
February	142,831	133,600	122,410	122,878	143,397	183,444
March	319,460	210,892	169,946	265,041	186,159	376,554
April	255,710	376,482	350,389	243,289	407,096	470,824
May	408,418	360,055	348,347	397,282	348,697	512,021
June	364,507	478,493	361,140	297,636	385,848	413,025
July	526,574	392,045	452,558	412,586	401,985	635,358
August	672,024	587,676	642,582	576,594	573,259	693,310
September	466,255	348,865	355,108	363,545	391,700	530,421
October	289,102	251,183	281,378	299,130	361,896	510,905
November	182,251	160,771	179,981	197,123	213,255	317,746
December	181,696	176,844	174,775	182,623	190,981	350,632
Total	3,997,386	3,668,541	3,624,361	3,551,750	3,816,528	5,239,132

Month	1973	1974	1975	1976	1977[b]
January	424,498	415,762	549,359	472,953	491,773
February	273,854	278,524	352,497	333,908	395,691
March	413,891	435,011	753,993	498,389	578,580
April	796,893	746,720	557,904	824,229	961,748
May	565,809	542,317	784,283	617,005	924,957
June	762,385	754,196	575,152	778,791	780.746
July	729,420	700,971	785,873	871,827	1,142,611
August	934,587	843,884	904,457	760,295	834,852
September	713,585	683,801	683,366	655,280	910,346
October	541,610	558,261	592,475	733,885	1,000,001
November	373,440	404,692	432,080	451,726	489,780
December	303,469	412,855	425,359	427,753	531,207
Total	6,833,441	6,776,994	7,396,798	7,426,041	9,042,292

a A West Berliner is defined as a person carrying personal identification papers issued either by West Berlin or West German authorities.

b These statistics were not available after 1977.

TABLE IV

Travel by East Germans (Who Are Not Pensioners)
to West Germany – excluding West Berlin

	1973	1974	1975	1976	1977
January	3919	2450	2397	2666	2280
February	4216	3220	2771	2681	2709
March	4372	3180	2967	3424	2917
April	3325	3980	3592	3753	3878
May	3014	4094	4272	4914	4213
June	2380	2901	3123	3286	3413
July	2879	3169	3118	3581	3586
August	3223	3017	3289	3510	3955
September	3507	2922	3806	3889	4046
October	4191	3442	3959	4218	3853
November	3456	2881	3543	3575	3661
December	3016	3042	3605	3254	3322
Total	41,498	38,298	40,442	42,751	42,733

[a] This figure could be slightly higher since it is sometimes difficult to distinguish between genuine cases of family emergency and pensioners, which come under a different category. These statistics are not publicly available after 1977.

approximately 48,000 nonpensioners from the GDR traveling to the FRG on urgent family matters.)

In 1964 East Berlin agreed to allow older, pensioned people to visit the West on the grounds that, if they defected, the state would seize their remaining pension and property (which is legally questionable) and on the sounder rationale that older citizens tend to return to familiar surroundings anyway. These figures in Table V are therefore partially inaccurate because they also include some "would-be pensioners" on emergency family visits. Nonetheless, they reveal three consistent pat-

TABLE V

Visits by Pensioners from the GDR to the FRG and West Berlin

| 1965 | 1,218,825 | 1967 | 1,072,496 | 1969 | 1,042,191 | 1971 | 1,045,385 |
| 1966 | 1,055,498 | 1968 | 1,047,359 | 1970 | 1,048,070 | 1972 | 1,068,340 |

Month	1973	1974	1975	1976	1977
January	29,342	35,483	45,133	44,071	45,174
February	33,465	51,017	61,686	63,332	71,366
March	60,275	79,510	93,284	83,755	93,685
April	100,979	116,596	113,291	119,621	123,022
May	145,362	170,350	162,463	160,050	154,419
June	138,335	138,528	128,581	142,019	130,841
July	143,170	141,219	143,946	139,233	135,805
August	163,122	156,419	156,694	147,446	150,396
September	153,211	148,606	150,564	151,152	151,203
October	126,450	120,221	119,366	118,494	113,746
November	79,304	74,841	71,981	75,346	74,496
December	84,851	83,216	85,400	83,798	84,551
Total	1,257,866	1,316,006	1,330,389	1,328,317	1,328,704

| 1978 | 1,384,118 | 1979 (January–June) | 634,914 |

terns. First, the pensioners seemed to have been unaffected by the constraints of the retrenchment years; a relatively constant number came out each year. Second, after 1973, the figure increased by roughly 300,000 and remained relatively constant in 1974. Third, visits triple in the summer when travel is more convenient. The program has worked relatively satisfactorily for the GDR. It has partially reduced tensions over family separations, provided a continuous channel for consumer goods and FRG deutsch marks, and minimized the adverse ideological influence on the youth. It has proved to be reliable (since 1970 an average 10,000 East Germans have been allowed to exit legally and remain abroad, including emigrants, freed political prisoners, pensioners, and, recently, those who have been expelled).

Tables II-V are incomplete because of a change in the reporting procedures and tabulation format that make comparisons more difficult and tedious. Comparisons of the new categories, however, confirm the conclusions. In July 1978, 1,783,512 West Germans and foreigners travelled to and from West Berlin; in July 1979, 1,967,851 made the trip by all means of transportation. This is a 10.3 percent increase. Between January and July 1978, 10,612,554 visitors went to and from West Berlin. Between the same period of time in 1979, the figure was only 10,565,441—a .4 percent decline. In July 1978, 436,197 West Germans and foreigners travelled to and through the GDR to third countries; in July 1979, 436,197 made similar excursions—a 7.4 percent drop. Between January and July 1978, the figure for this category was 2,119,364; from January to July 1979 it was 2,063,378—a 2.6 percent decrease. Furthermore, the figure for daily excursions in the border area during this period dropped 14.3 percent, while the daily excursions for West Berlin remained relatively constant at around 1.4 million. The Berlin Senate estimates that the number of West Berliners travelling to East Berlin under regulations governing Berlin visits has dropped slightly from 3.4 million in 1976 to about 3.2 million in 1979. The number of East Berlin pensioners visiting West Berlin and the FRG during the period of comparison fell 3 percent and in July, 4.5 percent. Possibly, most indicative of new trends, East Berlin cut the number of travel permits to the FRG for family emergencies by 30.5 percent, from 5097 in July 1978 to 3541 in July 1979. These figures suggest that virtually all forms of personal travel between East and West Germany are declining, some dramatically.

The figures in Table VI uphold the opinion that more mail is sent from the GDR than is sent to it. Since 1968 there has been consistently heavier traffic from the GDR with an up-turn after the *Grundvertrag*. It peaked at 136,600,000 letters, and then dropped in 1972. There are nearly 80 times more West Germans visiting East Germany than vice versa, and direct communication obviously has made letter writing less necessary. (However, these figures include both official, business, and professional correspondence; no breakdown of personal mail has been made public.) Furthermore, the GDR was slow in installing new telecommunications (see below), requiring hours of delay and discouraging, until recently, the use of this means.

TABLE VI

(Letter Mail Excluding Registered Letters and Parcels)

Year	To the GDR and East Berlin	From the GDR and East Berlin
1968	106,800,000	116,400,000
1969	110,800,000	113,600,000
1970	121,300,000	124,800,000
1971	124,600,000	124,700,000
1972	103,600,000	124,400,000
1973	100,100,000	123,900,000
1974	83,900,000	124,900,000
1975	81,000,000	136,600,000
1976 [a]	76,900,000	99,700,000

[a] Statistics on postal deliveries are no longer publicly available.

Finally, letters remain both cheaper and more precise than telephone calls.

Before access to East Germany was eased most parcel post packages consisted of gifts. The flow understandably was often four times higher from West to East. After personal visits from the West became more common, the number of parcels sent to both countries decreased. Now most packages are commercial items.

The growth in telecommunications is more difficult to present in tabular form because of incomplete statistics, the different levels of automation and type of equipment. The following tables, however, may provide an overview.

Table VII

Parcel Post Traffic

Year	To the GDR and East Berlin	From the GDR and East Berlin
1968	42,700,000	18,400,000
1969	39,200,000	10,600,000
1970	41,900,000	13,900,000
1971	38,100,000	12,200,000
1972	40,900,000	10,800,000
1973	34,300,000	13,100,000
1974	32,400,000	8,200,000
1975	29,000,000	6,900,000
1976 [a]	27,900,000	8,700,000

[a] Statistics on parcel post traffic are no longer publicly available.

TABLE VIII

Long-Distance Telephone Lines ^a

Date	West East	West Berlin East Berlin	Total
Until 1970	34	none	34
Mid 1970	40 new	none	74
Mid 1971	74	30	104
End 1971	60 new	120 new	284
Mid 1972	48 new	51 new	384
Mid 1974	40 new	201	423
Mid 1975	56 new	240 new	714
End 1977	90 new	12 new	821
End 1978	72 new	48 new	941
End 1979	84 new	36 new	1061
End 1980	84 new	36 new	1181
End 1981	84 new	36 new	1301
End 1982	72 new	48 new	1421

^a All telephone users in the FRG can direct
dial to East Berlin. By the end of 1978,
77 percent of the calls to the GDR and to
East Berlin were self-service. Since April
1975 calls from West Berlin to East Berlin
were fully automatic. By the end of 1978,
97 percent from West Berlin to East Berlin
and GDR were direct dial.

In 1969 there were 34 switchboard-operated lines between
the FRG and West Berlin and GDR. There were none between
West Berlin and East Germany. These lines carried 962,000
calls; slightly more than half originated in the West. By 1972 the
calls increased to 1,292,000, again with 60 percent coming from
the West. In 1971 30 semiautomatic lines were installed between West Berlin and East Berlin and the GDR. Over one
million calls were placed by the FRG and 806,000 by West

TABLE IX

Increase in Telephone Calls between
the FRG and the GDR [a]

Date	West–East	West Berlin–East Berlin	Total
1968	500,000	none	850,000
1969	500,000	none	960,000
1970	700,000	none	1,290,000
1971	1,800,000	800,000	–
1972	5,100,000	2,900,000	–
1973	5,800,000	2,800,000	–
1974	6,100,000	2,700,000	–
1975	9,700,000	3,800,000	–
1976	11,300,000	6,300,000	–
1977	12,800,000	7,200,000	–
1978	16,700,000	8,300,000	–

[a] Total summations cannot be determined accurately
since automatic calls cannot be registered. These
figures represent overall line usage, rather than
a total of individual calls and suggest only
relative increases.

Berlin. Table VIII indicates the addition of new lines. By 1976, there were 5,100,000 calls placed by the FRG to the GDR, of which 1.25 million went to East Berlin and 1.23 million were placed by West Berlin to the GDR. In addition 6,163,000 calls were made between East and West Berlin. Berliners (both East and West) also made six million calls outside the two Germanys. By 1978 an estimated 16.7 million calls were made between East and West Germany and 8.3 between the two Berlins; a decade of substantial growth.[130]

There are no statistics on the percentage of the calls that have been private. Presumably most have been commercial and in some way official. Nonetheless, the telephone and human voice have helped relieve personal tension and frustration and improved the overall efficiency of inner-German cooperation. The mutual advantages on this "new connection" were underscored by a joint statement agreed in October 1977 to project completions of 1421 lines by 1982.

Telegram and Telex facilities are now providing more service than in 1970, when there were 24 nonautomatic telegram wires between the FRG and the GDR, plus four between West Berlin and the GDR. By the end of 1971 there were 67 and 19 automated wires respectively. (Two more were installed in 1974 in West Berlin.) Telex facilities were increased from 35 transmitters in 1970, servicing the FRG and GDR and 11 servicing West Berlin-GDR traffic, to 91 and 35 respectively in 1972. Since then there has been no known effort to increase either sets of facilities, indicating mutual satisfaction that a former problematic issue area has been cooperatively resolved.

INNER-GERMAN TRADE

For political reasons, based on the one-nation theory, Bonn has successfully persuaded the European Community that the GDR should be regarded as an extension of the FRG and, for matters of trade only, should be granted by the EEC the same customs status as African members of the French Union. This has proved psychologically more valuable than it has commercially. GDR trade with the FRG has consistently remained about 10 percent of its total volume. This is largely due to an interest-free credit now amounting to 850 million DM annually, repayable in two years. (GDR debts to Bonn are now estimated at $1.6 billion above the credit allocation.) Openings to the EEC have gradually increased GDR trade with the EEC to less than 20 percent of its total.

East Berlin's new interest in the West is not due to its technology licenses, industrial investment goods, and producer goods alone. It is due to the fact that credit is available. The GDR now owes Western banks an estimated $5.2 billion. This deficit and growing economic difficulties, however, have discouraged the East Germans from applying for more. Trade with Western countries other than the FRG has dropped as much as 50 percent in three years, emphasizing the renewed importance of inner-German trade as a source of badly needed commodities by the GDR. The tables in Annex B provide both a background and an overview and comparison up to the present of trade development trends. Tables X and XI, however, deal with the period after the *Grundvertrag* and should be analyzed separately.

Several observations can be made. The 22.3 percent rise in overall trade from 1973 to 1974 was not unprecedented, but it was an expected increase after the retrenchment years. Growth rates have been irregular since then, in part because of an unsettled market in the West, due to recession, followed by recession in the East. The cutback in credits and sales by other Western states is likely to be reflected in a modest temporary upturn in trade between the FRG and the GDR. Some West German economists maintain that trade growth rates, however, are likely to stagnate into the 1980s largely because of an indefinite slowdown in the GDR economy.

Trade in specific goods is not given by the tables. However, the percentage of total export trade in iron and steel products dropped from 12.9 percent in 1974 to 8.8 percent two years later, although the mark value actually increased, indicating a shift in basic priorities and increased costs. Chemicals peaked in 1975 at 813 million DM or 18.7 percent of total exports and then dropped to 747 million by 1977, but then returned to 810 in 1978. This decline is reportedly temporary and was due to the opening of alternative indigenous sources and lower prices for CEMA products. Machine-building equipment and tools constituted roughly 20 percent of total exports, reaching 964 million DM in 1978. Electronic products were next at only 3 or 4 percent, or 189 million DM. With only minor fluctuations,

TABLE X

West German Exports in Inner–German Trade (1000 DM)

	1974 DM	1974 %	1975 DM	1975 %	1976 DM	1976 %
Agricultural and food products	353	9.7	335	8.5	381	8.9
Raw materials and producer goods	1947	53.	1918	48.9	1739	40
Industrial investment goods	810	22.1	912	23.3	1251	29.3
Coal and minerals	114	3.1	369	9.4	479	11.2
Consumer products	414	11.3	339	8.6	367	8.6
Miscellaneous	33	.8	49	1.3	52	2
Total	3671	100.0	3922	100.0	4269	100.0

TABLE X (Continued)

	1977		1978		1979	
	DM	%	DM	%	DM	%
Agricultural and food products	429	9.8	46	1.1	37	10.1
Raw materials and producer goods	1674	38.6	1804	44.0	176	48.2
Industrial investment goods	1335	30.8	1430	34.9	76	20.8
Coal and minerals	487	11.2	373	9.1	39	10.7
Consumer products	366	8.5	393	9.6	32	8.8
Miscellaneous	49	1.1	55	1.3	5	1.4
Total	4340	100.0	4101	100.0	365	100.0

Source: Warenverkehr mit der Deutschen Demokratischen Republik und Berlin (Ost), Fachserie 6, Statisches Bundesamt, Wiesbaden. Also "Die Entwicklung des innerdeutschen Handels," Bulletin (March 15, 1979).

TABLE XI

West German Exports in Inner—German Trade
(1000 DM)

	1974		1975		1976	
	DM	%	DM	%	DM	%
Agricultural and food products	555	17.0	501	15.	665	17.1
Raw materials and producer goods	1282	39.4	1217	36.	1491	38.5
Industrial investment goods	323	9.9	340	10.2	421	10.9
Coal and minerals	113	3.5	89	2.7	115	3.0
Consumer products	960	29.5	1075	32.1	1162	30.0
Miscellaneous	19	.7	120	4	23	.5
Total	3252	100.0	3342	100.0	3877	100.0

TABLE XI (Continued)

	1977 DM	1977 %	1978 DM	1978 %	1979 DM	1979 %
Agricultural and food products	642	16.2	582	14.9	56	15.6
Raw materials and producer goods	1518	38.4	1499	38.5	148	41.2
Industrial investment goods	452	11.4	428	11.0	42	11.7
Coal and minerals	129	3.2	115	2.9	9	2.5
Consumer products	1183	30.0	1247	32.0	96	26.8
Miscellaneous	29	.8	28	.7	8	2.2
Total	3953	100.0	3899	100.0	359	100.0

Source: Warenverkehr mit der Deutschen Demokratischen Republik und Berlin (Ost), Fachserie 6 Statisches Bundesamt, Wiesbaden. Also "Die Entwicklung des innerdeutschen Handels," Bulletin (March 7, 1979).

exports of consumer goods have remained relatively constant over the last ten years, despite the fact that the borders have been opened. The most significant change was made in trade for coal and minerals, with a jump from 119 million DM, which was 4 percent of the total exports in 1973 to 487 million or 11.2 percent in 1977, with a slight, temporary downturn in 1978. Clearly the energy crisis forced a major revision of the GDR's import plan. East European energy sources are relatively cheaper, but more in demand. West German coal is likely to be imported to a much greater extent by the GDR at the expense of other commodities that might be needed directly to accelerate growth.

The imports the FRG receives are primarily meat poducts in the agricultural category. Consumer goods importation has been relatively constant, commanding roughly 30 percent of the total import trade, with textiles the major component. GDR iron and steel products have remained competitive over the past several years with Western products, and East German chemicals have held their own on the West German market, one of the world's leading chemical manufacturers. Finally, mineral oil now accounts forr roughly 13 to 15 percent of the total export trade. Over the past five years the patterns of imports by the FRG have not fluctuated seriously. Yet imports over the long term have been less stable than exports, suggesting that some contracts may have been politically inspired, both to ease balance of payments problems and also the domestic economic difficulties of the GDR.

While Bonn may remain sensitive to the GDR's economic difficulties, there are clearly upper limits to the levels of credit it can extend and the imbalance of payments it can sustain. Trade may be restricted further because of the lack of new or better quality commodities. But Bonn is faced with its own domestic economic difficulties and with far greater problems within the industrialized world than it faces with the GDR. Thus, Bonn has probably approached the upper levels of its trade with the GDR and, therefore, one means that is frequently considered to be an infallible instrument for achieving international cooperation, interstate commerce, might not function so well in the future to stimulate inner-German cooperation.

A final aspect of inner-German trade is freight traffic and the changing modes of transportation.

Surveying truck traffic first, Table XII indicates that the number of West German trucks carrying goods into the GDR increased steadily from 2376 in 1970 to 5900 in 1976. The number of West Berlin trucks that went to the GDR increased from 24,556 in 1970 to 53,640 in 1974 and dropped sharply to 11,300 in 1976. The number of West German trucks delivering goods from the GDR to the FRG rose, in much larger numbers than those entering East Germany, from 6,463 to 16,000 by 1976. West Berlin trucks returning from the GDR also increased, but not as dramatically, from 33,592 in 1970, to 49,113 in 1974, back to 38,500 by 1976. In contrast, the number of East German trucks transporting goods into the GDR rose from 25,896 in 1970, to 47,630 in 1974, and back to 40,200 in 1976. And the number of East German trucks traveling from the GDR to the FRG climbed from 86,866 in 1970 to 118,600. (Note! These figures do not include traffic between the FRG and West Berlin.)

The relatively small number of West German trucks (less than 5 percent) and the sharp decline in the number of West Berlin trucks delivering goods to the GDR were the result of both political and economic reasons. Truck import tonnage doubled (see below) but the number of trucks did not; this suggests that there was a rapid conversion to larger vehicles. More importantly, the sharp discrepancies between the numbers of trucks exporting and importing goods indicates that both Germanys (especially the GDR) are afflicted by a large proportion of inefficient one-way hauls. This could be a significant area for coordination and improved cooperation, especially since the number of East German trucks in use is more than double that of the FRG and West Berlin.

Tables XIII and XIV deal with all modes of transportation and indicate differing patterns where tonnage, not merely numbers, are included. FRG exports by rail rose and then dropped by 40 percent in one year, yet imports by rail expe-

TABLE XII[a]

Freight Transportation by Trucks

(numbers of loaded trucks, without West Berlin traffic)

Year	West German Trucks entering GDR	West Berlin Trucks entering GDR	West German Trucks exiting GDR	West Berlin Trucks exiting GDR	East German Trucks entering FRG	East German Trucks exiting FRG
1970	2376	24,556	6463	33,592	25,896	86,866
1971	2925	31,485	7904	35,634	28,817	103,200
1972	3533	42,400	9845	40,988	36,947	111,281
1973	4359	41,852	10,757	44,123	43,053	109,784
1974	5088	53,640	10,796	49,113	47,630	108,786
1975	5089	30,830	13,236	43,750	41,957	109,055
1976	5900	11,300	16,000	38,500	40,200	118,600

[a] The collection of this data was stopped in 1976.

Source:
Güterverkehr der Verkehrszweige, Fachserie 8, Statistisches Bundesamt, Wiesbaden; and Statistische Mitteilungen des Kraftfahrt-Bundesamt, Flensburg.

[115]

TABLE XIII

Freight Tonnage between the FRG and the GDR

FRG Exports

	1975	1976	1977	1978
Rail	4,691,018	6,091,783	3,782,416	3,720,453
Truck	60,973	55,735	56,670	56,271
Barge	1,746,014	1,737,182	2,067,871	2,861,278
Seaship	574,646	756,926	396,399	149,619
Total	7,072,651	8,641,626	6,303,356	6,787,621

TABLE XIV

FRG Imports

	1975	1976	1977	1978
Rail	5,662,140	6,559,234	6,932,670	6,007,578
Truck	150,615	235,600	277,670	302,493
Barge	1,901,074	1,810,257	1,656,240	1,437,028
Seaship	7,051	80,900	19,319	11,545
Total	7,720,880	8,685,991	8,885,899	7,758,644

Source: Güterverkehr der Verkehrszweige, Fachserie 8, Statistisches Bundesamt, Wiesbaden, and Statistisches Mitteilungen des Kraftfahrt-Bundesamt, Flensburg.

rienced only minor fluctuations. This discrepancy was reportedly due to the slowness in reloading the cars on the East German side so that West German rolling stock was unduely idled. Truck export tonnage remained roughly the same, but import tonnage doubled up to the mid-1970s. This increase was apparently required because of the drop in tonnage conveyed by other modes. Barge export tonnage increased by roughly 40 percent, again partially making up for declines in conveyance by other means. Yet barge import tonnage declined modestly. Seaship export and import tonnage dropped sharply to 14 percent of the 1976 figure within two years. While the figures were modest compared to total tonnage, such a sharp decrease was due primarily to financial reasons; it was simply more economical to utilize shipping elsewhere.

Many of the changes in the modes of transportation were the result of politics and economics. Other changes stemmed from purely technical reasons such as the processing of rolling stock. Yet the field of transportation is potentially one of the most mutually rewarding areas of cooperation. As economic recession begins to afflict both Germanys, commercial incentives may increase to the point that greater coordination may emerge.

Since inner-German trade is stagnating, what then are the prospects for future cooperation? While there have been remarkable increases in the use of some means for cooperating, such as West-East travel and telecommunications, there has also been a decline concerning some questions such as pollution control. On issues such as cultural exchanges and legal matters, there has been almost no substantive progress. From these confusing patterns several points seem to emerge. First, the apparent inconsistencies in overall developments and interactions are a reflection of the present nature of the relationships with the superpowers as well as of the state of East-West German political relations. Thus cooperation will depend on a general and localized improvement in the climate of détente. A better political atmosphere seems unlikely in the near term.

Second, there was no grand design for the improvements that were made during the period between 1972 and 1979 and none has emerged. There was only a list of mutually understood grievances, not a comprehensive program defining the spectrum of cooperation. These weaknesses on both sides were a result of a variety of factors, including alliance politics, the unpredictability of super power interactions, the independent activities of private business in the FRG with the GDR trusts, and the largely defensive, reactive nature of GDR behavior toward Bonn.

Finally, the central issue for both sides politically, the level of human contact, has apparently raised a point understood by both East and West Germans, although it is not considered satisfactory by either society. The plateauing in West-East travel was voluntary. The increase in telecommunications was a logical compensation. But the East German goal of gaining formal and personal West German recognition of its independent sovereign status has not been fully met, and the long-standing FRG aim of improving the quality of life for the East German also has been partially achieved.

Chapter V

The German Problem in The Broader East-West Context: Consequences for Western Policy

EVOLUTION IN THE CONCEPTUALIZATION AND CONDUCT OF
SOVIET FOREIGN POLICY

An assessment of the implications of the on-going German problem for Western policy makers should appropriately be placed within the the broader context of East-West relations, before examining them within the narrower perspective of inner-German affairs or even regional European interactions. Such an appraisal can be facilitated by first analyzing the evolution in Soviet foreign policy, the role of strategic parity in systemic stability, and the nature of the special great-power relationship before considering the future of inner-German relations.

The Soviet stance on the German problem and European stability must be considered to assess the prospects for improved regional relations. Yet Moscow's German policy is only a single factor in its comprehensive global perspective and policy. The Soviet Union has a number of interests and objectives dictated by its geographic position and its perceived role in the world. Among these, it seeks to prevent formation of hostile coalitions and preclude isolation, contain and neutralize the influence of the United States, that is, counter the objectives of the United States to achieve global stability and, organize the world, to its advantage, into expanding clusters of "progressive" states (a modified conception of the Tsarist notion of geographic spheres of influence). The Soviets also expect to promote the political legitimization of the eastern half of Europe and the Finlandization of Western Europe, (that is, achieve local accommodation of Soviet interests, self-censorship and restraint, and international acceptance of this relationship).[131] Likewise they want to neutralize Japan and contain, but preferably gain some accessibility and thereby influence over, China. Finally the Kremlin must avoid wars that could endanger the development of socialism by systematically expanding its armed forces to the point where it can achieve its most likely maximum aim, that is, Finlandization over selected areas through the mere perception by these dependencies of its power, rather than through the exercise of military threats or coercion.[132]

Under Khrushchev, the Soviets crossed several strategic thresholds. Their previous policy of holding Western Europe hostage for the good behavior of the United States was augmented by the development of limited strategic nuclear capabilities, but they were only able to achieve a minimum deterrence posture against the continental United States. Yet this dual threat to the United States was sufficiently potent to encourage Moscow to adopt a higher risk-taking policy of challenging Western interests in various regions of the third world. But then Moscow was challenged by the unorthodoxy of Chinese policy. As a result, Khrushchev endorsed national communism and destalinization in Europe to gain sufficient cohesion on his Western flank so that he could focus greater attention by socialist countries on China. More than any other factor, the dilemma between defining the limits of socialist orthodoxy and the outer perimeter of nationalist aspirations led to Khrushchev's ouster and, paradoxically, to China's adoption of its own separate road.

Even before Khrushchev's demise, however, changes in Soviet policy were perceived. Unable to establish acceptable conceptual or practical definitions of national communism with Yugoslavia and Rumania, Khrushchev was forced to drop his plans for making Eastern Europe economically more viable and thereby politically more cohesive.[133] After 1963, the proposal to establish supranational planning in CEMA was abandoned, without providing alternative guidelines for needed economic reforms or for further political destalinization. Soviet East European policy began to drift. Then, the Cuban missile crisis demonstrated that Soviet overseas strategic capabilities were limited. As a result, in 1963, Moscow adopted the position of accelerating arms control talks with the United States (the Limited Nuclear Test Ban was signed in August 1963), expanding its overseas airlift and naval capabilities, and abandoning its minimum deterrence force for a posture of strategic parity.[134] At the same time, Moscow reviewed its third world policy and accepted more rigorous, efficient criteria for economic aid that severely lowered its involvement in "nonessential" states.[135] Finally, after the Cuban debacle failed to achieve the aim of demonstrating that the Kremlin was the true center of world revolutionary forces, Moscow was forced onto the defensive.

Brezhnev took power in October 1964, amid the mounting pressure from Peking and the retreat elsewhere, which placed constraints on the new leadership. As a result of this, the general consensus during the initial years was that the new leaders were a "fumbling, bumbling" mediocre collective, incapable of new drives.[136] The lull in foreign policy was not due to indifference, however, but also to an internal stabilization process. Khrushchev had created such chaos and insecurity in his frequent party and government reorganizations that in the 18 months preceding the 23rd Party Congress key ministries were reunited, one-half of the Central Committee department heads were removed, and the powerful Party-State Central Committee was abolished, all before Brezhnev received the title of General Secretary.[137].

By the end of 1965 Brezhnev was able to make important changes in foreign policy matters that provided the basis for a new set of initiatives which marked the opening of the Brezhnev era. Sufficient progress had been made on the nuclear nonproliferation treaty (although agreement was being blocked by other states rather than the United States and the Soviet Union). Also, missile technology had been advanced to the point that Moscow was prepared to seek parity with the United

States. Finally, the Chinese no longer challenged the Soviets, at least for the time being. Peking had overextended itself, and its embassies and news offices were being closed in various third world countries for alleged subversion. In the aftermath, Peking virtually suspended its foreign policy and turned inward into the Cultural Revolution. Thus the Soviets formulated four initiatives which established the priorities for the next phase of the Brezhnev era. At the December 1965 meeting of the Warsaw Pact Political Consultative Committee, Brezhnev formally launched the United Action campaign against American bombing of North Vietnam, although China remained vehemently opposed to any concerted action for any cause because of the dangers of enhancing Soviet hegemony. The campaign soon became a worldwide effort to aid Hanoi and eventually played a major role in the communist victory. Equally important it deepened the Sino-Soviet dispute by demonstrating that the Kremlin indeed had the leadership capability to organize the world revolutionary forces into viable international drives against China's expressed interests and deliberate counteractions.

In January 1966, the Kremlin seized the opportunity of the Indo-Pakistani War to convene a summit conference in Tashkent and to mediate a successful agreement. The further extension of Soviet prestige into the subcontinent, evidenced by the Kremlin's interest in stability, and subsequent Soviet efforts to further regional cooperation were viewed by China as a manifestation of Russian encirclement. While Peking had regarded Soviet inroads into South and Southeast Asia since 1955 as detrimental to Chinese interests, it was now unable to respond decisively. Moscow was moving to the offensive on this front, as seen in Brezhnev's call in 1969 for an anti-Chinese security pact.

At the March 1966 23rd Party Congress, Brezhnev announced an additional plan: a new European policy embodied in the call for an all-European security conference. The Final Act, signed ten years later, was not a quasi-peace treaty to codify Soviet hegemonic gains since World War II, as Moscow intended. It did contribute, however, to the conclusion of the

Ostverträge and the *Grundvertrag*. But this new initiative has ultimately served as an important constraint on the implementation of Moscow's European initiative through the emergence of national communism, known as Eurocommunism, and rising dissent within the Bloc.

In May 1966, Kosygin visited Cairo and rejuvenated Soviet Middle Eastern policy by attempting to organize a cohesive block of "progressive" Arab states that could demonstrate sufficient collective strength to gain the initiative on the Palestine question.[138] The long-term benefit (until 1973) was to raise Soviet prestige and influence in the Middle East to an all time high. The immediate effect, however, was the creation of a diplomatic drive for a political solution which evaded Soviet control and erupted in the June War. Moscow then recognized the opportunity for entrenching its influence by guaranteeing Arab military parity with Israel as the basis for equality in the bargaining process. Yet Soviet involvement in the Middle East fueled concern in Eastern Europe about the danger of Soviet overcommitment and the intensification of hegemony. The reactions of intellectual circles indirectly contributed to Novotny's and later Gomulka's downfall and to subsequent Soviet efforts to compartmentalize its foreign policy (see below).[139]

In 1969 and 1970 Brezhnev made new gains through his foreign diplomacy. The Rumanian and later the Czechoslovak resurrection in favor of national communism versus Proletarian Internationalism had been decided on Moscow's terms. Soviet respectability in the Middle East was registered by the acceptance by the United States of Moscow as coresponsible for peace and an invitation to participate in the two-power talks. Progress was being made in arms control with the approval of the United Nations. Preliminary talks had commenced on a peace settlement in Southeast Asia. Major advances were made on the numerous negotiations related to the "normalization" of East-West European relations. Finally, the USSR was constructing 250 ICBMs annually.[140] The net effect on these diplomatic and military advances was the decision to participate in the SALT talks, the first attempt by the great powers to deal with issues germane to their vital interests and, there-fore, a major step towards détente.

But, after 1972, Moscow tilted toward a more "confronta-tionist" stance. First, it ignored the responsibilities of con-straint required in the Vietnam Peace Treaty. Then, despite limited improvements in East and West German and in East and West Berlin relations, it took a tougher stand on the legal connection between West Berlin and Bonn that has obstructed further progress toward improved relations between the FRG and GDR.

More critical, Soviet combat forces were expelled from Egypt in July 1972 because its pledge to insure military parity could not be fully met without the delivery of "decisive wea-pons" that would permit the resumption of hostilities. In the winter Moscow recognized the vulnerability of its influence in the Arab world and compromised. It agreed to Sadat's de-mands to supply sufficient weapons to wage a war for limited aims. Even partial success, however, would require surprise and deception. Moscow accepted the risks to détente of another war and deliberately concealed its role in the Arabs' preparations. This was a flagrant violation of the underlying provision, contained in the May 1972 Basic Principles that were to govern great power behavior, which explicitly state (Articles Two and Three) that each power will not seek unilat-eral advantages and that both will do "everything in their power so that conflicts or situations will not arise which would serve to increase international tensions or impending crises."[141] Soviet duplicity in the October War was regarded as adequate justification for the exclusion of Moscow from the settlement process and the curtailment whenever possible of its influence in the Middle East.

In the meantime, SALT II was launched, but amid mounting evidence that agreements guaranteeing "essential equiva-lence" were being disregarded by the Soviet Union. It was developing four new ICBMs which would presumably be MIRV-ed, greatly magnifying the advantages the Soviets al-ready enjoyed under the Interim Agreement.[142] Soviet goals in strategic affairs were gradually coming to be regarded by Washington as being ambiguous or deliberately misleading; perceptions that were reinforced by the Soviet performance at the MBFR Talks.

It is difficult to assess the reasons that the Soviet Union shifted toward a tougher line. While the Kremlin was comfortable about the outcome on some issues and dissatisfied with others, the balance was positive. The 24th Party Congress asserted that the aggregation of historic forces now favored socialism in every sphere, economic, political and military—a more convincing assertion in 1971 than when Khrushchev made the same claims in 1956. The positive political gains mentioned above, coupled with the introspection in the United States over the Vietnamese defeat and the worst political scandals in American history, and the unilateral advantages the United States gained by its China policy, may have prompted the conclusion that a selectively more assertive foreign policy would not invoke unacceptable risks as in the *coup de main* in Angola and intervention in Ethiopia and Afghanistan.

Yet this newly found Soviet confidence was constrained between 1973 and 1978, because Soviet efforts to organize a cohesive block of progressive African states around Angola, the Rhodesian confrontation states, and Ethiopia have yet to meet the test of time (there is little evidence that Soviet influence in southern Africa is no less susceptible to the volatility of regional politics and the reversals it experienced earlier in the Congo, Ghana, Mali, Egypt, Sudan, Somalia, and Algeria). The dilemma over supplying the Arabs decisive weapons and seeking a durable basis for Soviet authority in the Middle East had compromised its credibility in the settlement process and reduced Soviet influence in the region to one of the lowest points.[143] The oil embargo had an adverse impact on the world economy, including the Soviet system (accompanied with other economic shortfalls, these difficulties led in 1976 to a form of "socialist recession" and forced the Soviet bloc to seek loans from the West, worth, in 1979 to be an estimated $60 billion.[144] Mao died in September 1976, but relations were not

improved between China and the Soviet Union. The model of
Proletarian Internationalism and the perennial dilemma of pre-
scribing both the conceptual character and pragmatic extent to
which national communism should be tolerated sustained the
broadest setback yet at the June 1976 conference of European
communist parties (legitimization for Western communist parties prescribes compliance with traditional norms of political
responsiveness, guidance, and accountability, not exhortation,
mobilization, and coercion—by 1978 Moscow had temporarily
won the argument). Finally, SALT and MBFR talks offered
little hope for achieving the types of limitations and mutual
constraints envisaged by the United States in 1972, creating
growing apprehension in the West about the Soviet military
buildups and political intentions. The aggregation of these
developments denied the United States the opportunity to
formulate a proper basis for its much-heralded "generation of
peace." A disillusioned Secretary Henry Kissinger finally
characterized détente as a "permanent confrontation."[145]
Small wonder that since 1976 the Soviets have shown increasing concern that the ideal of détente might be jeopardized and
that the "normalizing process" might be impaired.

What conclusions can be drawn from the general survey
about the conceptual evolution of Soviet foreign policy under
Brezhnev? One, made in earlier times, has been that foreign
policy could be used advantageously to deal with issues rather
than a single problem, as in the Khrushchev period. In the
1950s the Soviets pressed alternatively on various issues: Berlin, Turkey, or Quemoy. Moving in specific directions at given
times or until unacceptable resistance developed, it exploited
the natural advantages of a centristic power, especially as it
became defensively assertive. The advantages of dealing with
a single issue is that of initiative and offense against a pluralistic
opposition concerned with a variety of constraints. The development of Brezhnevian foreign policy towards a foreign policy
dealing with multiple issues represents a major change in Soviet perceptions of its role in the international system and the
nature of the adversary relationship. Moscow now has an

interest in and bureaucratic capability to deal simultaneously with a wide range of issues that often compete domestically. However, this type of diplomacy could eventually force the Soviet Union to accept greater international stability since it permits the West to insure good behavior by linking agreements on various issues.

To overcome this problem, the Soviets adopted the innovation of compartmentalizing issues.[146] That is, after the adverse East European reaction to Soviet Middle Eastern policy in 1967 and 1968, Moscow recognized that effective pursuit of a foreign policy devoted to a number of issues requires a high degree of compartmentalization to prevent adverse effects from one set of issues influencing another or from one region to another. For example, at the December 1969 Pact summit conference Moscow encouraged its allies to pursue bilaterally their respective grievances against the FRG on the apparent grounds that if they could be induced to remain "little Europeans" they would have little interest in Soviet issues elsewhere. (As a result, there was no known negative East European reaction to the deployment of Soviet combat forces to Egypt in 1970 or to Afghanistan in 1979 and, despite the implications for the Pact, there were no known public top-level consultations.) Compartmentalization has been most effective when applied to issues concerning regional areas, but not on issues concerning interparty affairs. As a result, changes have been made to deal with interparty affairs. Since 1968 there has been a simultaneous narrowing and broadening of Soviet tolerance levels towards its allies. Soviet tolerance has been constricted by more precise ideological controls.[142] To do this, it has strengthened its military posture, accelerated regional integration, and increased dependency on the USSR for raw materials. However, the Soviet Union has become gradually aware of the necessity to accelerate the modernization process of all socialist states, including itself, thus permitting wider East-West contacts. For example, between 1960 and 1972 trade between Eastern Europe and the West gradrupled from $3 billion to $12 billion. Broader contacts required the Soviet Union to accept the gradual modification of the socioeconomic structure of Eastern

Europe such as the differences in the improvement of the standard of living in East Germany as opposed to Rumania.

At the expense of being repetitious, the conduct of Soviet foreign policy can now be characterized by the establishment of conventional spheres of influence to consolidate its authority, not as instruments for regional penetration. The Soviet Union has most often organized "progressive blocs" of likeminded states with interests common to its own as the means for regional penetration or expansion of Soviet interests. The concept, if not the precise term, of proletarian internationalsim still governs Soviet tolerance for national deviation and the scope and pace of change among ruling communist parties. The concept of peaceful coexistence also still governs the Soviets' terms for the level and nature of its engagement in the international system. The aggregation of these policies strongly suggests that the Soviet Union remains relatively comfortable and confident under circumstances of "permanent confrontation."

The Brezhnev era, then, has the properties of continuity, consolidation, and cautious expansion. Moscow has consistently viewed diplomacy as a process, not an end, and bargaining as a series of agreements gained in its favor. It has intensified its stakes in the international system, confident that to do so would promote peaceful coexistence (which it has dogmatically defined as allowing competition on issues, but not on values). It has steadfastly held that deterrence has a political as well as a military application, namely the neutralization of resistance to Soviet policy. Soviet diplomacy has been most effective when it has operated against minimum uncertainties and less so when confronted with unexpected contingencies. Probably the most distinctive features of Brezhnevian foreign policy have been its rationality and adaptability to conceptual change. It is difficult to determine whether these features were due to the man (a consensus politician), growing bureaucratic politics, or changing international influences. The gravest concern for the future, however, is that Soviet foreign policy under a new Brezhnev might lack this innovative adaptability and lapse into more brittle, dogmatic policy which was followed during the years of confrontation.

THE GERMAN PROBLEM IN THE EAST-WEST STRATEGIC
CONTEXT–PARITY AND SYSTEMIC STABILITY

One of the most difficult problems the West has had to deal
with is to determine Soviet military capabilities and political
intentions accurately. Indeed, estimates by the United States
of Soviet power and perceptions of Moscow's objectives in
international crises have often been erroneous.[148] An underlying rationale minimizing asymmetrical American and Soviet
strategic advantages was that political leverage against the Soviet Union was difficult to correlate directly with strategic nuclear weapons. There was no danger that marginal increases in
power by either side could be converted into significant political influence. During the 1960's it was argued that the political
utility of American strategic weapons systems could best be
extracted indirectly: by demonstrating restraint while maintaining a position of unquestioned strength. The lack of political convertibility of strategic nuclear weapons to political
power was cited later as the justification for finally relinquish-
ing the strategic superiority of the United States.

The difficulty with such rationale was that it did not fall
within the "scientifically binding laws of strategy" governing
Soviet defense planning. Indeed, Moscow ignored the entire
relevance of restraint and attached a high degree of political
value to nuclear weapons and strategic forces. When technology and resources have been available, the Soviets have in-
vested in programs designed first to deter and then to match the
capabilities of the United States. Minimum deterrence force
have been systematically upgraded and military parity with *all*
potentially hostile forces has been a deliberately established
goal.

Thus, the United States misperceived not only Soviet technical and industrial capabilities to match American force postures, but it also erroneously calculated the political utility
Moscow attaches to strategic equality and possible superiority.
The Soviets have gone beyond the theory the United States
held in the 1960s that political rewards could be earned by
exercising restraint from a position of strength. They argue that

the credibility of military power depends upon the willingness and ability to use force when it serves one's own interests.[149] The upgrading of their capabilities was demonstrated between 1975 and 1978 when Moscow successfully intervened in Angola and Ethiopia; a similar operation in the Congo 15 years before had been effectively blocked by the United States. Also in 1975 the USSR constructed a major military complex in Somalia; similar efforts in Cuba five years earlier had been decisively challenged by Washington.[150]

From a doctrinal viewpoint, the Soviets have apparently concluded that if military force has been effectively demonstrated, the imposition of subsequent constraints will be politically more more persuasive. In other words, the old adage is still applicable: Opponents must be convinced of the risks they will incur if they threaten to use military force to gain political ends. Also, from this position of enhanced strategic strength, Moscow can be expected to conduct a more flexible foreign policy that may, when necessary, include an increased willingness to accept risks if challenged or to be more assertive under favorable circumstances, as it apparently calculated in its invasion of Afghanistan.

In the technical sense, the Soviets have not yet achieved military superiority over the United States or the West; rather they have attained parity marked by disparities and persisting physical constraints, such as assured access to strategic oceans. More important, it has successfully used its military power to gain American recognition of its political equality with the United states.[151] This is now seen as probably the most important single achievement of the Brezhnev era. The very magnitude of this success underscores the importance, from the Soviet viewpoint, of the relationship of strategic parity to political coexistence and the desired level of "crisis stability."

Three main developments contributed to the degree of stability presently known as the special great-power relationship between the United States and the Soviet Union, rather than détente. The first was the nature of anticipated change in the international system and its components or subsystems. Lenin's original injunctions about coexistence and the subsequent conduct of Soviet foreign policy was based on the fundamental assumption that the "correlation of historic forces" would eventually revolutionize the entire system, component by component.[152] The countervailing sweeping changes proposed in the immediate postwar era by both the East and the West stimulated the stalemate that characterized the cold war. It was not until East-West relations finally were destalemated in the early 1960s that the prospects for realistic changes began to emerge. Paradoxically, frustrations over achieving transformations of the international system led to mutual acceptance of the central features of the status quo. This transition "from détente based on change to détente based on the status quo" led to the thaw in East-West relations.[153] In Willy Brandt's terms, the best way to change the status quo is to accept it and thus provide a framework for mutual accommodation.[154]

The second contributory factor to the special relationship was the change in political structures within both blocs. The most important changes have not occurred between the two camps, but rather within both. These changes were the products primarily of indigenous conditions and to a lesser extent to external stimuli from East-West interactions.[155] Clearly, the nature of the modifications within the two subsystems differed. In the East, the principles and practice of democratic centralism and integration were reinforced under Soviet hegemony; in the West, pluralism was reaffirmed, but traditional conflicts were only partially resolved. Both East and West, however, also witnessed the simultaneous broadening and narrowing of their foreign policy objectives. In the East the fissures created over the German problem generated individual, but coordinated, efforts to settle national grievances with Bonn and to develop commercial contacts with the West. Yet the instruments of Soviet control were steadily strengthened. In the West, on the other hand, the *Ostverträge* were designed to open the way for wider and more varied relations with the East as well. Yet the multilateral negotiations at MBFR, CSCE, and the Common Market created renewed, and on some issues, unique solidarity within the pluralistic West. The broadening and narrowing of foreign policy aims created both the opportunities and reassurances necessary for the special relationship to function, even within the constrained dimensions of the early 1980s.

The third pillar of the special relationship was the Soviet achievement of strategic parity. As mentioned above, parity with disparities is the underlying stabilizing factor in great-power relations; it has become the "equalizer" in the fragile balance between the world's most industrialized society and the leading developing nation. Of the three causal factors that have led to the attempt to achieve détente, military parity is the most important; it is the most sensitive and susceptible to national security interests. It was not until the United States acknowledged Soviet strategic parity that the other two factors in the special relationship could be applied to alter the adversary relationship and that issues affecting vital national interests could finally be raised for negotiation. The preservation of parity thus has become the "self-regulating" mechanism in the stability of the special relationship. Any inequality in strength can reasonably be expected to be refined or offset. But any unilaterally perceived significant change in the strength of the other side might cause the one to feel threatened and possibly jeopardize the stability of the relationship. Firmer underpinnings for the relationship are desirable based upon greater understanding of individual political interests and mutually acceptable standards for the behavior of the great powers.

ROLE OF CONSTRAINTS

There are two basic theoretical concepts involved in the continuing differing viewpoints of the two sides over strategic arms limitations. The United States has consistently maintained that the overall objective of arms controls should be the assurance of "crisis stability" and "essential equivalence." These concepts prohibit either opponent from developing a unilateral military advantage that would tempt it to launch a first strike by exploiting the mutual understanding that both will be permitted to continue modernization of military forces.

They also offer an alternative formula for pegging security to exact equality in each weapons component, which has had a stimulating effect on arms competition. Both concepts were formulated to provide realistically assured security, survivability of forces, and ultimately reductions in strategic weapons.

The Soviets have rejected these concepts because of the alleged disadvantage they suffer in their geostrategic position. They have insisted on "equal security taking into account geographic and other considerations."[156] That is, the United States is surrounded by friendly states and open oceans. But the USSR is surrounded by potentially hostile threats from China and Europe. Therefore, prudent Soviet security policy requires that Moscow's total forces equal the aggregated strategic strength of China, France, West Germany, Britain, and the United States. A weaker force might tempt blackmail or aggression on either or both fronts—an argument rejected by the United States.

Future arms control agreements are likely to become increasingly dependent upon mutual political confidence. The stress on the political approach will be made primarily by the West to compensate for the decline in confidence since SALT I and the beginning of the MBFR talks, and the emergence of questions about Soviet political intentions, especially after the invasion of Afghanistan. Political trust is also becoming increasingly imperative since the technical means for national surveillance are not completely reliable in identifying technological progress in weapons development. Prudent policy prescribes that the balance between crisis stability and the essential equivalence be maintained by the continual development of military options, on the one side, such as the Precision Guided Munitions, Theater Nuclear Modernization, and regional Cruise Missiles, and the continued search for negotiated arms controls, on the other side. The decision of the December 1979 NATO Council was to seek the reduction of major offensive systems, such as curtailment of the SS-20 mobile missile, cuts in tank forces, and reduction in tactical nuclear war heads. Preserving the balance between weapons modernization and pursuing arms accords is plausible if there is a general understanding of the necessity to reduce the scope and nature of the respectively perceived offensive threats and that confidence can be established in the improbability of surprise attack. It is in these two categories that political reassurances generate the most credibility.

Both SALT and MBFR talks face uncertain futures because of events in Southwest Asia and mounting opposition within the United States Senate and growing public concern about the scale and quality of Soviet modernization of its strategic and theater forces, which is clearly discernible. This new climate was evidence by public opinion polls wherein, for the first time in 20 years, 46 percent expressed the view that the United States should be "superior" to the Soviets in military strength and that too little was being spent on defense (74 percent endorsed higher taxes—up to $10 billion a year in new military programs—and 64 percent believed that the Soviets would not live up to their part of a new SALT accord.[157] It is, as yet, clearly too early to assess the durability of the opposition, but the Senate amendments to the SALT II Treaty along the lines advocated by Senator Nunn and Henry Kissinger will significantly increase defense spending by the United States in the 1980s.

SALT also has faced opposition in the Soviet Union, at first because the Soviet leadership was at a distinct impasse due to Brezhnev's health. He was still too powerful to be ignored and yet too incapacitated to make the necessary concessions for outright endorsement by the United States.[158] Washington has frequently sought to negotiate around difficult problems concerning strategic arms hoping through dialogue to "educate" Moscow about the dangers inherent in "arms racing."[159] But, at the time, the fear of weapons obsolence was discouraging the pursuit of this policy. The Navy had declined to a low of 460 ships (accompanied by heavy curtailments in future procurements). By 1985 the United States will have a land-based ICBM force of no more than 650 older generation Minutemen III. (If the Soviets continue to modernize existing ICBM systems and those under development, they could enjoy a six-to-one advantage in useful payload and possibly a numerical advantage in reentry vehicles.) Finally, the B-1 was cancelled without a reciprocal Soviet concession or the provision of an adequate alternative. Under these circumstances, there is likely to be adverse effects on American threat perceptions, arms-control negotiations, and domestic pressures within the United States to correct the anticipated imbalances.

The emphasis on establishing political confidence is stressed by the "interactionists" who perceive that stability will be maintained if the great powers continue to compete for influence over third parties. Indeed, the rivalry may become more intense as the continutally divergent social aspirations preclude the convergence of political values and motivations.[160] Under these circumstances, stability will depend increasingly on political confidence, which the West interprets as a balanced exercise of restraint and the disavowal of attaining unilateral political advantages. This viewpoint was stated in the 1972 Basic Principles that were to govern the special great-power relationship. While the overall aim was the self-denial of unilateral quests for advantages, the operative provisions of the Basic Principles dealt explicitly and implicitly with the issues of warning, surprise, and duplicity.[161] As mentioned above, the interpretation by the United States was that political confidence and a stable relationship would prohibit unexpected and potentially uncontrollable moves that might be misperceived as a bid for unilateral gain. Increased cooperation would require sufficient communications to preclude surprise or the suspicion of deceit. The seeming violations of the principles of warning and constraint against opportunism and the mutual disregard for the Basic Principles lowered the focus of both sides to the less lofty problems of compliance and enforcement.

After the age of innocence passed for the Carter Administration, political confidence no longer rested on the notion of self-regulation, but reverted to the sounder concept of reciprocity and interrelating agreements on negotiable issues. Political constraints could no longer be presumed to be an inherent characteristic of the special relationship. Constraints would have to be negotiated or induced. One of the most encouraging distinctions between the cold-war era and the present is that both constraints and reciprocity can now be more fully discussed.

THE NATURE OF THE SPECIAL SUPER POWER RELATIONSHIP

Uwe Nerlich has pointed out that the conceptualization of the special great power relationship has undergone distinctive changes on both sides.[162] Indeed, three separate phases can be identified. The first phase was characterized by the view that the concept imparted profound, sweeping changes in East-West relations. These dramatic changes merely prescribed some form of transition without definitive end results or objectives. Modifications were envisioned only in existing international structures, such as SALT, to provide a more durable base for "the generation of peace." This dramatic view of the concept prevailed, during the 1960s, primarily in the West until specific negotiations on security matters provided the evidence for a new perspective—the second phase.

In the second phase of the interactions, the negotiating process itself and the respective bureaucratic decision making mechanisms assumed importance; greater stress was placed on the continuity and controllability of the negotiation process. Rather than substituting structures, this view required the creation of complementary communications channels for existing ones. Nerlich calls the latter perspective the *"consensual* view of détente" and concludes that it is now the prevailing opinion.[163]

But Nerlich points out that the weakness of this understanding of the relationship is that it focused on the negotiation process and its formal results as ends in themselves and failed to consider the political forces responsible for the bargaining. Furthermore, by stressing newly created structures, such as SALT and MBFR, it ignored other, more routine means for bringing about agreements, such as those used to make the grain transactions between the United States and the Soviet Union. Finally, some of the new organizations (notably CSCE and MBFR) failed to produce the level of substantive results commensurate with the collective efforts to get them organized. Thus, because of the dramatic conceptualization of the negotiations, high priority became attached to the symbolism inherent in any East-West interaction. This symbolism, in turn, became an end in itself and added confusion about the true state of the present degree of change taking place in the "abnormal normalization process," to use Egon Bahr's term.

While phase one was characterized by a premature "overselling" of the pentagonal structure of peace, phase two can be seen as a vigorous pursuit of negotiations, partly for their own sake, that overstated the limited scope of the bargaining and observed the nature of the interdependence between the Soviet Union and the United States. Indeed, a third phase may emerge wherein stress may be placed on the accurate prescription of the nature and limits of interdependence.[164]

A central feature of the "dramatic" phase of détente was the rise in Western expectations that a fundamental change could be made in the special relationship. This was evidenced in the "consensual" phase where the creation of a steadily expanding web of agreements would serve as incentives and penalties to insure mutually acceptable behavior.[165] The difficulty with this theory arises from the question of validation. For example, it cannot be decisively demonstrated that more pressure from the United States on the Soviets during phase two would have produced greater concessions (as asserted by Kissinger's detractors). It is equally difficult to prove that the Soviets would have behaved more aggressively or assertively during the economic "crisis of capitalism" between 1974 and 1976 without the constraints of the special relationship. Validation is problematic because of the question of determining the precise value one side attaches to any given interaction or unilateral move and in insuring that these values will not change unperceived over time. Thus, the effectiveness of the incentives and penalties will remain an accurate reflection of political perceptions of adversary intentions—a task not satisfactorily achieved during phase one and two.

The highest Soviet foreign policy priority still is to manipulate the relationship for the advancement of the "historic forces.'' Correspondingly, the main Western aim is to contain any advance and reduce the level of confrontation. The challenge for future relations is to devise concepts that can reliably moderate great power behavior. The West enjoys several means of influencing the evolution of the relationship, such as a larger, more reliable economic base, rapidly expanding technologies, compatibility of commercial and fiscal policies, similarity of social and political values shared by many Third World countries, and the devolution of the international system from bipolarity to multipolarity.[166] Individually or collectively, these are important levers.

The Soviet Union, on the other hand, is no longer the vanguard of the economic revolutionary forces that were to prescribe the model for economic and social development. By the nature of its economic system and its products, flawed by technological and bureaucratic deficiencies, it participates in none of the international organizations attempting to conceptualize, organize, and establish the emerging new international economic order. Real power cannot be distinguished from the setting in which it must be exercised. In the increasingly interdependent new order, self-sufficiency is inefficiency, yet the exercise of power is now the capacity to reshape the system so as to minimize undue dependencies and vulnerabilities among all nations. This remodeling requires the authority to compromise and make concessions. But the Soviet Union remains dependent, vulnerable, and largely beyond the pale of the transformation of the system. It is, therefore, susceptible to pressures from both the West and the South and compelled to accept rather than manipulate or formulate the changes that will define the characteristics of the international system in the 1980s—crucial leverage, indeed, if used prudently.

Chapter VI

Prospects for Further East-West German Relations Within Broader Strategic and Political Contexts

In light of the continuing "limited super power adversary relationship" or "permanent confrontation," equal security remains the basis for regional stability and progress toward mutual political accommodation. East-West German relations should now be assessed within the context of broader East-West strategic and political problems. The present strategies of both Germanys and their allies set as minimum goals the denial of those aggressive or offensive options which appear sensible from both military and political viewpoints and which one estimates the opponent considers justifiable to risk (conceivable losses balanced against anticipated gains). Yet the political intentions and the credibility of either side's military strategy cannot be accurately assessed, providing latitude both for uncertainty and suspicion, and for initiating measures to promote political confidence. If, as suggested above, real power cannot be distinguished from the setting in which it must be exercised, the Soviets should have only marginal apprehensions. Their military posture in Eastern Europe, and the GDR particularly, is superior to that of opposing forces in almost every category of weapons systems.

Security on both sides depends on two fundamental concepts: The first is the rationale of deterrence in central Europe, whereby the use of military force offensively is deemed irrational, and, therefore, its credible application under present military postures is regarded as rather improbable. Nonetheless, until recently, local deterrence seemed firmly based on the assumption that the great powers would retaliate strategically against any attack. With the advent of strategic parity, however, this assertion became less a matter of political reassurance and strategic analysis about the conditions for and implications of a massive exchange. Retaliation has become increasingly contingent upon the abstract calculus of national decision making, not purely strategic appraisals, and upon the manipulation of the uncertainties of a major war, and hence on the presumptions of the opponent's risk calculations.[167]

Given the present force postures, it appears that Moscow and East Berlin regard central Europe as a highly sensitive region within which the margin for testing the readiness of the United States to escalate a conflict under acceptable risks is rather narrow.[168] Thus, deterrence in central Europe has assumed a new rationale, whereby military force is likely to be employed primarily to achieve psychological dominance and political dependence—a goal that has so far proved to be mutually exclusive.

Second, the concept of security focuses on the assessment of détente discussed above. It suggests that positive political effects can be achieved by the exercise of self-regulation or the imposition of constraints. The importance of this is that self-regulation and constraints remain the basic alternative to military posturing for mutual security, stability, and further accommodation, if not interdependence.

There are at least two theoretical components of the concept of interdependence: normalization of relations and interaction. Normalization of relations is the prerequisite for cultivation of extensive interactions between states. From the legal viewpoint normalization can be defined as the establishment of harmony between the norms of international law and the actual state of affairs. This harmony can be resolved by either reshaping the facts so that they correspond to the norms or altering the norms in their application so that they correspond to reality.[169] With the *Ostverträge* and the *Grundvertrag*, the FRG formally abandoned its earlier rejection of the legality of the partition and insistence on reunification based on the norms of

self-determination. Instead of gaining normalization by changing factors created in defiance of legal norms, Bonn has accepted the reality of the existing international order, as well as
the political respectability and legal accountability of the rival
state. Thus, a legal normalization of relations has been established which has permitted growing interactions.

The second component is the nature of the interaction. Interaction includes any type of social contact—political, economic,
and cultural. The extent of the contacts depends upon supply
and demand, or deliberate constraints, or specific preferences.
The interdependence of East and West Germany is based on
mutual and reciprocal interactions, based on conditions of legal
normality, and selected shared national interests and goals. It
is limited by countervailing dependencies or individual national
priorities. This interdependence is reinforced, moreover, by
reciprocity for infractions against agreed norms and commitments, by mutual benefits for continued participation, and by
self-inflicted penalties for withdrawal from or curtailment of
any interaction.

Statistics provided in Chapter IV and in Annexes A and B
indicate that a marked increase has occurred since 1972 in the
number of interactions.[170] Yet interdependency has not been
visibly strengthened in direct proportion. This deficiency is due
in part to the *differences in the ability of both Germanys to
apply reciprocity or constraints*. The GDR is still politically
insecure, as is suggested by the recent indications of social
dissent and unrest (see below). One interpretation of the spas-
modic, nervous government reaction is that East Berlin was
signalling Bonn that increased interactions had not produced
dependencies but that East Berlin remained independent at a
time when dissidence was spreading in Eastern Europe in the
wake of the Helsinki CSCE Conference, and that the FRG
itself was still vulnerable to unilateral actions.

The Federal Republic indicated that it could increase the
extent of its interaction when it continued to try to improve the
welfare of East Germans, increasing its trade and commercial
benefits even during the recession of 1974 and 1975. Support
for bettering the East German living standards has provided

Bonn with a political advantage over East Berlin, but it must be sustained even under adverse conditions to preclude counter-productive public criticisms.

The improvement of human rights and well-being is likely to remain the most significant measure of the improvement in German interdependence. (It also will reveal the degree of improvement in overall East-West European relations.) One of the most important results of the CSCE Final Act was the unexpected encouragement it provided for human rights and reformist movements that, in turn, cemented renewed solidarity among the ruling elites in East Germany, Poland, Czechoslovakia, and the Soviet Union. (Between 1972 and 1973 ten bilateral treaties were signed among Pact members to provide greater policy coordination and institutional cohesion on the "ideological front" than existed during the height of the cold war, indicating that the East Europeans were hypersensitive to the subversive potential of CSCE.)

The outcome of the negotiations on "Basket Three" was the West's rejection of the Soviet demand for universal endorsement of the status quo in Eastern Europe. Western insistence upon provisions for the freer flow of people and information was firm evidence that it expected social change and modernization to occur in Eastern Europe and that it wanted an appropriate role in formulating the direction and pace of those changes. The West was *not* calling for political subversion or even for another Prague experiment. It wanted a more precise definition of the function it should play in ameliorating human welfare that would also be acceptable to the Soviets under the Brezhnev Doctrine and Socialist Internationalism. How could the West, for example, participate in technology transfers and grant extensive commercial credits as the East expected from Basket Two without risking an unprovoked rise in public expectations? The Socialists insisted on defining their own conditions for *Abgrenzung,* while domestic dissidence has proliferated.

Thus a second set of characteristics of interdependence mentioned earlier—vulnerability versus dependence—are assuming more tangible forms in the GDR and Eastern Europe. As these states gradually increase their dependence on the West for technology as a means of raising labor productivity, they increase their vulnerability. Both, as a result, become detrimental to the expansion of interdependence. Yet the socialist goal of self-sufficiency represents inefficiency in a rapidly modernizing world which lacks the mutually agreed specialized division of labor. Thus, there appear to be definite barriers to the level of interdependence that the Socialists are prepared to accept; they seem prepared to opt for continued inefficiency and the accompanying social unrest. This choice imposes constraints on the West's understanding and expectations about normality. An additional barrier to interdependence is the divisibility of the German nation, that is, the viability of the concept of two states in one nation as opposed to two separate and distinct nations. The degree of national identification and distinctiveness will partially determine the future level of interdependence between the two entities (see below).

The two Germanys have now existed longer than both the Weimar Republic and the Third Reich combined. Yet, as Ralf Dahrendorf has observed, there are few historical examples of a society changing so fundamentally in so short a time as has West Germany. Indeed, there are equally few examples of a nation changing so quickly into two almost diametrically opposed directions as have the two Germanys.[171] There are similarities in these profound developments, yet discernible differences. The economic miracle achieved in West Germany is well known and thoroughly documented. As the strongest economy in Europe, the FRG successfully steered the European Community through the international recession following the energy crisis. It has convincingly shifted Community attention from further political integration to emphasis on the importance of achieving transnational harmonization of domestic policies to regulating inflation, unemployment, and currency policies, among others. Indeed with trade surpluses that have ranged from $22 billion in 1975 to $10 billion in 1977, Bonn's economic weight has produced powerful political influence.[172] One of the most decisive factors that has kept the leftists only on the verge of power in France and Italy for the past several years has been the knowledge among the moderate voters that communist-dominated governments in these two countries would inevitably challenge Bonn's attempts to harmonize national economic policies, and possibly disrupt existing trade patterns, create payments crises, downgrade existing commercial advantages and levels of prosperity, and even could compel these countries to become debtor nations.

Probably more important for the long term has been the political miracle the Federal Republic has achieved. All responsible West German political parties opted for integration and rehabilitation in the West, which meant the adoption of the democratic processes of representative and responsive government. The Republic's institutions have been strengthened by the periodic transfer of power from majority government to various coalitions and by the recent challenges of economic recession and urban terrorism. After the political assassinations of prominent West German officials and industrialists, alarmist statements were raised abroad about the rise of "Hitler's children." The government replied with wide-ranging legislation "to improve law and order, without jeopardizing our liberal principles." (Yet civil liberties remain restricted for extreme leftists in many states.) Nonetheless, the FRG has emerged as one of the most politically stable major European states.

After the end of the forced reparations extracted by the Soviet Union and the erection of the Berlin Wall, East Germany produced its own economic miracle. It did not have the advantages of the Marshall Plan and was endowed with only marginal quantities of raw materials. Yet by the mid-1970s, it was the ninth most-industrialized state in the world with the highest standard of living in the communist world.

Melvin Croan argues that in a sense there has also been a political miracle in the GDR. It has successfully broken out of the isolation imposed by the Hallstein Doctrine and achieved general recognition by the international community and the UN.[173] Domestically, the former "counterelite" of technocrats has effectively been absorbed into the party cadre through the demise of the older orthodox membership and the improved educational norms of the younger cadre.[174] But this seemingly remarkable consolidation within the governing elite remains tarnished by continuing legal and illegal emigrations, the use of exile to silence political opponents, the maintenance of *Abgrenzung,* and the strengthening of Soviet armed forces on GDR territory. Finally, the demands for internal reforms reportedly from within the party cadre suggests that there are rifts in an apparently unified elite (see below).[175] These problems complicate that of assessing the extent and nature of national identity and the conceptualization of the nation by the two Germanys. They also challenge the accuracy of claims to the DDR achievement of a political miracle. They underscore Peter Ludz's enjoinder that East-West German relations are marked by *both* cooperation and demarcation or *Abgrenzung.* The nature and scope of this demarcation warrants detailed examination, since it represents the primary constraint against further cooperation.

PROBLEMS OF SOCIAL ORGANIZATION, POLITICAL DISSENT, AND PARTY LEADERSHIP IN THE GDR

Since the Khrushchev era, Soviet East European policy has been governed by several delicately balanced, often contradictory, concepts: security and normality, national communism and Socialist Proletarian Internationalism, and cohesion and viability. All are perceived as stabilizing and legitimizing instruments.[176] In the latter case James Brown has commented that:

> Cohesion with viability has been the main Soviet aim in Eastern Europe since Stalin's death. . . . Cohesion is a situation where, in spite of local differences caused by variations in local conditions, there is a general conformity of ideological, political and economic policy, both domestic and foreign, as laid down by the Soviet Union in any particular period. By viability is meant a degree of confidence and efficiency, especially economic, in the East

European states that would increasingly legitimize Communist rule and correspondingly reduce the Soviet need for a preventive preoccupation with this region.[177]

Despite the retrenchment years, cohesion between the two had been largely restored with the ascension of Erich Honecker to party leadership. It was the erosion of the economic viability of East Europe and the GDR in the mid-1970s, however, that was the main catalyst in East German social disaffection and problems for the SED leadership.

The economic reforms incorporated in the 1963 6th SED Party Congress were basically, streamlined planning, aggregated production plants or units (VVB), and adjusted prices. Also, the number of indices for efficiency were reduced. While these reforms carried the GDR through the slump in the mid-1960s that hit other Socialist countries, namely Czechoslovakia and later Poland, they created numerous adverse social complications without achieving economic priorities. First, the main goal of the reforms was to be a major increase in consumer goods production comparable to the levels in FRG: "to catch, but not surpass." When these targets were not reached, a demoralizing impact was inevitable. Some questioned the morality of using "enemy" economic practices as models for socialist development; others retreated into social and political passivity or even economic criminality. Second, wages seemed to have been arbitrarily fixed or were determined by variables beyond the worker's control, such as lack of spare parts, or deficits in raw materials. Third, a primary factor in the reforms was renewed emphasis on the "scientific-technological revolution," which was to increase labor productivity and reduce manual labor. But the material benefits went primarily to the intelligentsia, not the blue-collar workers, exacerbating already existing class privileges and differences. Fourth, because of the heavy investment in new technology-intensive factories, shift work was required in order to reach profitability and efficiency standards. Shift work met strong resistance, despite special incentives, because it interfered with family life and reduced the opportunities for "moonlighting." Furthermore, shift work did not relieve the economic problems endemic to the system, including supply bottlenecks, insufficient transport, and an inadequate service structures.[178]

The Reform Program (NÖSPL) was expanded in 1965 into the Economic System of Socialism. The party recognized that the goals of increased industrial productivity had been only partially fulfilled but also had generated pressing social problems. As the economic situation worsened and the threat of social alienation increased, especially among the youth, and strikes and riots broke out in Poland, the 14th Plenum of the Central Committee formally abandoned the reforms and returned to centralized planning.[179]

The abandonment of the reforms had important psychological and political implications for inner-German relations. The reforms represented an explicit attempt to establish an East German identity, to demonstrate to other socialist countries that East Berlin had created its own separate road to socialism, and to indicate to the world that it was separate and distinct for its own specific reasons from the other German state. The deterioration and eventual termination of the reforms coincided and probably reinforced the retrenchment in foreign policy during the same period. The hardening of the GDR's position on *Deutschlandpolitik* may have been a direct consequence of the psychological let-down over the failure to demonstrate convincingly an authentic East German form of national communism. In compensation, East Berlin reemphasized the priority of gaining Bonn's full political recognition of its statehood.

After Erich Honecker became First Secretary on May 5, 1971, a gradual purge took place over the next two years of the leading economic reformers, insuring that the recentralization program would proceed unmolested. At the same time he strengthened the party's position by curbing the powers of the state bureaucracy.[180] Likewise, he abandoned ideological innovations and unattainable goals; for example, the "scientific-technological" panacea was quickly dropped.

But after the worldwide rise in raw-material prices in 1973 and 1974, the GDR suffered a sharp cost increase from which it has yet to recover. By 1975, 25 percent of the GDR's GNP was derived from its export trade alone, the same percentage as the FRG. But East Germany is much more dependent upon raw material imports and its industries are generally not as technologically advanced as those of the FRG.[181] Thus, between 1972 and 1975, total price increases for GDR exports were 17 percent, while prices for imports rose 34 percent. The GDR had shifted the share of its gross foreign trade with CEMA countries from 76 percent in 1961 to 65 in 1975 and from 20 to 31 percent respectively with the West; yet it experienced a $3.5 billion indebtedness to the West by mid-1976, and reportedly even greater trade deficits with CEMA countries, especially the USSR.[182]

By 1976 major changes were again introduced. The old reformers were reinstalled but without their reforms. Willi Stoph was again Chairman of the Council of Ministers and Gunter Mittag was again Central Committee Secretary for Economics. The planning apparatus was again strengthened, but the concept of profitability was weakened. The extent of plan fulfillment became the dominant measure again of economic performance. The reinstated leaders were expected to devise a more socially responsive plan. Their plan called for a 11 percent growth rate in foreign trade (actual growth in 1977 was 7 percent); and for investment only 2.1 percent (actual investment in 1977 was over 6 percent). Furthermore, price subsidization, with the discrepancies they create for the pricing system, were to be continued, especially for daily necessities.

This shift in economic priorities was partially motivated by the party leadership's awareness that social discontent was increasing despite the achievement of the highest living standards of any socialist country. The party acknowledged that there exists "no complete identity of interests of the society, of the collective, or of individuals." It was an uneven society that still retained "the birthmarks of the old society" and produced unsatisfactory results because of unequal opportunities and the inequitable distribution of proceeds of production.[183] This could hardly be denied, for housing remained critical, despite the construction of 100,000 new units annually. Class discrimi-

nation existed in education and cases of underemployment proliferated because of job reclassifications. Consumer product
subsidies for necessities in 1976 were 13 billion marks or 780
marks per capita. But the subsidies were raised by high turn-
over axes on nonessential goods and "luxuries," placing them
beyond reach of lower income earners. Most serious of all was
the influx of West German DM, accompanying the rise in West-
East travel. To absorb this second currency the GDR rapidly
expanded the number of Intershops, "Exquisit" and "Deli-
kat" shops, where primarily imported goods were sold. Indeed
the DM has become the *durable* currency of the GDR. It has
become the means for obtaining spare parts, signing contracts,
and even getting apartments repaired. In most cases this has
become the only way of gaining major improvements in the
quality of private life—the goal that now seems most important
to the average citizen. But these privileges are not the result of
productive output, skill levels, educational achievement, party
membership and loyalty, or other norms for the advancement
of socialism. These benefits depend upon whether one is fortunate enough to have relatives abroad or is in a position to
promote the interests of those who do.[184]

The DM has stimulated individuality, personal tastes and
interests, but also has eroded collectivity and a public sense of
pursuing common goals. It has also amplified existing class
fissures and created new ones. Moreover the DM has provoked
grave ideological discussions over such issues as the morality
of the use of unearned money (clearly an anti-Marxist, capital-
ist trait), the justness of a socialist work ethic, the necessity for
advanced education or skill levels, the purpose and utility of
party discipline. Indeed, it has challenged the underlying prem-
ises of the party's leading role. As a result, the SED has been
confronted, as has party leadership in Poland and Czechoslovakia, with the difficulties of dealing with growing pluralism
within a "collectized" socialist society and the emergence of a
latent dissent movement in the GDR. It has been the party
faithful, who normally have less access to DMs, who pressured
the East Berlin leadership, who, in turn, recognize the need for
hard currency, to introduce more exacting foreign exchange

regulations, which was done in May 1979. Under the new law, coupons are issued to recover DMs at Intershops, but East marks can be used to buy similar goods in "Exquisit" shops at roughly four times the normal price. Still Intershops earn 700 million DMs annually.[185]

Because of the nature of authoritarian societies and the continuing East-West standoff, the extent and character of the dissent is difficult to define, measure, and evaluate. It is even more problematic when crosscultural or historical comparisons are attempted. However, it appears that the GDR today, on the one hand, has learned the hard lessons other East Europeans have about testing the outer limits of Soviet tolerance for reform or autonomy, and recognizes that its security, even its political stature, is commensurate with the strength of the Soviet garrison. On the other hand, 15 Western news media services have permanent offices in East Berlin, in addition to periodically traveling correspondents, who cover major developments. More important 90 percent of the GDR can receive West German television and 100 percent can receive radio broadcasts. It is by far the most exposed socialist nation to Western influence.

The results of this exposure are ambivalent to assess for several reasons. No opinion polls are permitted and analyses must be based on personal contacts, media reports and direct indications of discontent. Nearly 55 percent of the population is under 40 years old. The average 35-year-old has limited scope for comparison. He can measure the improvement in his life style since the war and the material advantages he enjoys over his Soviet colleagues. Moreover he sees daily strikes, terror, dissension, unemployment, extravagance, and poverty in the West that is portrayed on West German television. In contrast, he sees the law and order, social benefits, and job security that the GDR enjoys on his own programs. Yet denial of freedom of travel in the West and the persistence of class inequities are usually ranked as the party's major shortcomings by this group, which apparently represents the numerical majority of the citizenry. This younger group is not seeking a fundamental alteration of the political system but rather modest material improvements, less class discrimination ("we-they"), and the recognized opportunity to travel. The younger generation is considered a largely apolitical society laying claims to more of the benefits of the twentieth century in comparison with the West Germans than their industrial prowess has theretofore extended.

There is, however, abundant evidence that beyond this rather amorphous element there are members of other segments of the society that can be identified more easily and have long espoused a political reorientation of the party guidelines toward true Marxist Social Democracy. Until recently this small group of individuals was confined to the intelligentsia. Within these groups, however, there are different forms of dissent with varying objectives, which have incurred a wide range of government responses.

In the first category—by far the largest (see Table XIV)—are those who voluntarily have chosen to leave the GDR. They include mainly legal emigrants who are granted exit visas primarily for humanitarian reasons, refugees who illegally escaped, and political prisoners who have been ransomed by Bonn. (Under the *Freikaufaktion* program, Bonn has paid over 100,000 DM for the release of over 8000 prisoners.) Of this total group of roughly 15,000 to 18,000, most have deliberately rejected the East German system, and in many cases risked their lives in doing so.

But the final expulsion in September 1977 of human rights activists Professor Hellmuth Ritsche from East Berlin and Dr. Karl-Heinz Nitschke from Riesa, Saxony, publicized a new trend. They had invoked the provisions of the Helsinki Final Act regarding an individual's right to choose his own domicile. By the end of 1976, 100,000 East Germans had applied for emigration visas. The government responded in 1977 with a campaign of harrassment of applicants, restrictions on Western travelers, police confrontations at the West German Embassy, the recall of the GDR Plenipotentiary to Bonn and, most seriously, renewed attacks on the status of West Berlin. These tactics proved ineffective, as the number of applicants reached 200,000 in 1978, and counterproductive since they only high-

TABLE XIV

Defectors versus Legal Departees 1967-1979

Year	Total	Defector	Percent	Departee	Percent
1967	19,573	6385	32.6	13,188	67.4
1968	16,036	4902	30.6	11,134	69.4
1969	16,975	5273	31.1	11,702	68.9
1970	17,519	5047	28.8	12,472	71.2
1971	17,408	5843	33.6	11,565	66.4
1972	17,164	5537	32.3	11,627	67.7
1973	15,189	6522	42.9	8667	57.1
1974	13,252	5324	40.2	7928	59.8
1975	16,285	6011	36.9	10,274	63.1
1976	15,168	5110	33.0	10,058	67.0
1977	12,078	4037	33.4	8041	66.0
1978	12,117	3846	32.0	8276	68.0
1979 (Jan.-June)	5671	1568	27.0	4103	78.0

Note that the defections in 1973 created reprisals against legal departees, and by 1978 the figure had not returned to the level of the early 1970s. Also between 1950 and June 1979, 3,092,548 East Germans settled in the West, 405,606 since the construction of the Wall, accompanied by 185 deaths along the border, 70 in the Berlin area. In addition, in 1978, 58,130 ethnic Germans from Eastern Europe and the USSR were resettled, 36,102 from Poland. The total reached 985,830 by June 1979. Under a separate accord, Bonn agreed to pay a lump sum settlement for claims by Polish citizens for pension claims against the Reich. Over 155,000 more Polish applicants must be covered by further negotiations.

Source: Bundesausgleichsamt, Bad Homburg.

lighted an embarrassing situation for the government. To apply for a visa by no means assured permission to emigrate, it merely registered a preference to leave, which the regime interpreted as rejection and inflicted personal penalties, such as social and economic reprisals. While the government coped with the first group with relative ease, this second group, of numerous applicants, sent noticeable tremors throughout the party leadership.[186]

The party changed tactics and focused on the hard-core intellectual dissenters, such as Wolf Biermann and Christa Wolf, who, among many others, had adopted the intellectual's role, common throughout Eastern Europe, of serving as the guardians of public morality and behavior. Through individual cases, studies, and portraits, the creative process was to raise new social and human questions, even if the intellectual could not solve them. The 11th Central Committee Plenum, held in December 1965, quashed such aspirations with the reimposition of a repressive cultural policy. However, the advent of a seemingly new era of détente encouraged this group again to become highly vocal. Unlike the first two groups, they were dedicated Marxists and determined to remain in the GDR, hoping to reform their society from within. Their demands were not material, but political. They insisted on the implementation of Marxist Social Democracy, that is, a participatory political organization which would insure unity between the masses and the party, guarantees that societal needs and political guidance could be harmonized, provisions for a society relieved of conflicts, discrimination, and privileges, and an economy planned to nurture and sustain social well-being.[187]

The regime sought first to isolate its critics and issued warnings and threats. It then adopted the Soviet practice of expulsion. The Soviets rationalize that if an intellectual is cut off from both the vital Russian soul and his audience, he will wither away. This has been true in most cases. But the German situation is different. Communication between the two states are extensive, and exile does not mean silence. In many instances it has meant intensified attacks on both systems. By 1979 several hundred reformists had been expelled without reducing the extent of criticism by East German writers published in the FRG.[188]

The exiled protestor was a new phenomenon in West Germany. For over 30 years Bonn had energetically pursued a policy of "gathering in the Germans," providing a welcoming haven for all ethnic Germans—a new home. But with the East German exiles, questions were asked: How far apart have Germans on either side of the border grown—not in terms of views and commitments, but in terms of experience and way of life? Can a person who has lived for two decades under socialism ever really feel entirely at home in the FRG? If a German exile in Germany feels a stranger, the thesis of two states in one nation may one day prove false.[189]

By 1978 the SED leadership was faced with more dissent, but this time by nonintellectual party members. In January an anonymous document of questionable authenticity was published in the West German weekly, *Der Spiegel,* entitled "The Manifesto of the First Organized Opposition in GDR: We are Against One-Party Dictatorship."[190] It criticized Stalinist practices, the aloofness of the top leadership, the abandonment of Marxist principles and socialist morality, economic failures, and persisting class distinctions, and demanded the introduction of a loyal political opposition and a reunified neutral Germany. Whether the document originated in East or West Germany, it reflected earlier comments by members from the middle ranks of the East German leadership, although some Western observers claimed the document indicated serious divisions within the top party leadership about more effective means of coping with all three groups and how to satisfy their most salient grievances. Whether accurate or not, the document was widely circulated in the GDR and apparently induced the leadership to resort to harsher countermeasures.

A more learned and scathing criticism of the GDR system was published earlier in August 1977 in the FRG by Rudolf Bahro, an economist, factory official, and party member since the age of 18.[191] Besides the standard criticisms of bureaucratic rigidity and the abuses of power, Bahro doubted that the Soviet-type elites are capable of internal reform. He called for the formation of a "New League of Communists" as a loyal opposition and the only means of genuinely fulfilling the emancipatory aims of Marxist socialism. Far more serious, he criticized the USSR for imposing the Soviet model for development on Eastern Europe, countries that have been traditionally Western oriented. "Neither in its substance nor in its shape or timing was it a consequence of an indigenous national development, but the result of an overwhelming Soviet participation in the anti-Hitler coalition and . . . of the subordination of the Communist Parties to Soviet state interests."[192] He advanced his criticism constructively by arguing:

In order to achieve a complete break-through to Socialism, their [these Western-oriented, East European countries] economic, social and cultural conditions require an institutionalized superstructure that can accommodate traditions very different from the Russian. What they need now, as does the Soviet Union, is . . . a readaptation of the superstructure . . . to stimulate simultaneous "national restoration, i.e., the reestablishment of national continuity with regard to various forms of social institutions. In the end, the problem is to adjust the institutions to the general form of (national) individuality, that is to the proper historical development.[193]

Besides Bahro's demands for the dismemberment of the bureaucracy, the elimination of the monopoly of information from the top, the gradual replacement of the ruling elites by the "New League of Communists," his espousal of a *Bund* of autonomous East European states pursuing nationally established values is dangerously close to the program that ultimately triggered the Pact invasion of Czechoslovakia.[194]

After giving an interview in August 1977 to FRG television elaborating his views, Bahro was arrested. In June 1978 he was tried and sentenced to eight years in prison. These terms represented a new harshness by the government to control criticism of the SED and the system. Bonn could not react "Carter-fashion" to alleged abuses of human rights by taking reprisals on other issues for fear that the GDR would curtail emigration, as occurred in 1974 and 1975. But Bonn did signal objection by rejecting feelers from the GDR for an East-West German summit meeting, following the hastily prepared and substantively inconsequential spring 1978 visit to Bonn of Leonid Brezhnev. With the imposition in July 1979 by the GDR of new repressive anti-Western laws, East-West German relations reached the lowest point in the years since retrenchment.[195] However, the challenge to the East German regime persists. There were minor street riots in October 1977 in East Berlin and in May 1978, and the continuing, if not increasing, socioeconomic problems suggest that the SED leadership is facing a renewed crisis of legitimacy. Its handling of the crisis is one of the principal criteria for determining the scope and character of future East-West German accommodation.

AUTHORITY AND LEGITIMACY AS CONSTRAINTS IN GDR BEHAVIOR

Without adequate empirical data, the section above has only been able to present social and economic problems in the GDR. The description portrays a society that is largely apathetic and indifferent, if not politically alienated. In spite of the Marxist-Leninist tenet requiring mass participation in the advancement of socialism, there has been a rapidly growing number of East Germans who have openly rejected the system or raised demands for its reform. This unexpected phenomenon has posed serious tactical questions for the regime; it has also raised fundamental issues about the nature of its authority and the legitimacy of its rule. Above all, the SED requires social stability, if not political respect, for the achievement of its goals.

Too often authority and legitimacy are regarded as synonymous. In some cases there may be such a coincidence, but in socialist countries this has not yet developed. This is partly because Marxist-Leninists deliberately rejected conventional Western norms for legitimization (the process of achieving the condition of legitimacy) and have substituted inadequate surrogates. Max Weber suggested that authentic legitimacy was possible in genuine revolutions under a condition termed "charismatic" legitimacy.[196] But the post World War II revolutions in Eastern Europe, as Bahro reminds us, were imposed by Soviet armed forces and remain within their present rough political parameters under the threat of Soviet intervention.

Seymour Martin Lipset argues that legitimacy is the function of interactions of specific sociopolitical groups who espouse specific values, as in the case of the socialist, communist, and fascist conflicts in the 1920s and 1930s.[197] But in a one-party system predicated on the concept of democratic centralism, there is little opportunity for alternative group organization and articulation.

Probably the most applicable model for legitimization of a divided nation has been provided by Gebhard Schweigler. He argues that indigenous legitimacy exists when the new political system is free of outside determination, the new system has attained success in the political and economic fields, and it proves to be better than both the preceeding system and the one with which it is competing in the other part of the divided nation.[198] Both Germanys failed to satisfy fully all three criteria, especially the East Germans. In their place, a consciousness of the nation-state was fostered that provided specific national self-images in both Germanys. Paradoxically the FRG has been more successful in cultivating a new self-image by deliberately avoiding nationalistic symbols and emotions; the GDR has consciously sought to foster them.

The most traditional Western notion of legitimacy is based on the participation of the citizens in some form of organized forum where correct norms are discussed and validated by vote. But this was explicitly rejected by Lenin as a remnant of bourgeois decadence. Instead, he and subsequent Marxist leaders sought other instruments: organization, socialization (indoctrination), coercion, incentives, ideology, and, in the case of the GDR, a national identity. These means have not achieved the desired results of genuine societal acceptance and support for common goals in any of the socialist countries.

Denied genuine legitimacy and an authentic national self-image, Marxists-Leninists have been forced to resort to instruments of authority, such as one-party rule, party hegemony, and democratic centralism in order to retain power. In light of the history of Eastern Europe since 1945 and recent events in the GDR, it is clear that national party elites place greater political priorities on social stability and party security; legitimization is an important but necessarily secondary interest. Legitimization cannot be abandoned or even ignored, especially in the GDR, where as a divided nation neither East or West Germany has achieved genuine "indigenous" legitimacy.[199] Both enjoy a "derivative" legitimacy (the GDR far more than the FRG) by virtue of their association with collective security systems, but they cannot progress much farther toward the indigenous form in light of the probably indefinite legal confrontation between the two states.[200]

In the 1960s the SED sought an *Ersatz* legitimacy based on future achievements to be accomplished by the economic reforms. But with the collapse of the reforms, the leadership was "forced to fight the battle with the weapons already in hand," that is, to gain public confidence and endorsement, albeit with an imperfect social structure and an inadequate economic system. In such situations, authoritarian parties are often caught in the dilemma of the abuse of its hegemonic power, risking further social alienation, or granting concessions necessary to restore public confidence, nourishing rising appetites. Moves in either direction are likely to erode or compromise its stature as the sole source of ideological doctrine, sagacity, and political authority.[201]

In every crisis in Poland, the party assumed responsibility for the public grievances and promptly attempted to engineer appropriate reforms within the party framework. In so doing, the Polish party was able to restore its authority and eventually its hegemony, only to be challenged again. (The Hungarian and Czechosolovak parties lost control of both the scope and pace of the reform movement.)

So far there is, of course, no such crisis in the GDR. But in light of the indicators of dissatisfaction and alienation, the SED has assumed no collective responsibility and has considered only minor alterations in economic investment plans. Initially, it concluded that the indicators reflect only personal grievances, requiring individual solutions, including the use of force. But, since July 1979, solutions were imposed on all of the people without making major concessions. Honecker is likely to ride out the immediate turmoil, despite West German press speculation to the contrary. This should not necessarily imply that the SED's authority will emerge untarnished. The challenge is likely to persist, however subdued, and may erupt unpredictably, as in the case of the spontaneous public outburst of enthusiasm for Chancellor Willy Brandt during the 1970 Erfurt summit meeting.

A central conclusion to be drawn from these circumstances is that, even after nearly 35 years in power, the SED cannot lay claims to indigenous legitimacy. Its political authority has been and is likely to continue to be questioned, despite a large cadre of devoted Marxist-Leninist party members. (It has a party membership of two million, mostly highly dedicated Marxists-Leninists.) But its persisting insecurity places limits on both the degree and nature of cooperation it will be able to engage in with Bonn, and the type of cooperation and level of pressure the FRG will be able to use in its inner-German policy.

FRG-US Relations: Changes in the Nature of the Special Ties

The FRG also has experienced insecurity, which has been a key factor in shaping its foreign policy over the past 30 years. It sought to overcome this through reconciliation with France and security guarantees from NATO and the United States. This effort to gain rehabilitation through integration with the West is now showing signs of change, primarily in Bonn's relations with Washington.[202]

Since the advent of the Carter administration, the former "special relationship" between the two allies began to erode. Carter kept his pledges to strengthen both in quality and quantity American forces in Europe, while demanding an unpopular

3 percent increase, in real terms, in defense spending by the NATO partners. But as the world economic recession persisted, he was blamed for malevolence and neglect on a variety of other issues that overshadowed the improvement in the American military forces in Europe.

The primary issue was the American "self-interest" in adopting policies to counter the recession. For the United States, unemployment was the most important problem; for the FRG it was inflation. When the Carter administration consistently refused to take measures to bolster the dollar and insisted on expanded West German economic growth, it appeared in Bonn that the United States was deliberately exporting its own inflationary policies under conditions dangerous to West Germany's export interests. Economics had become the primary bond, as well as obstacle, between the two partners.

Problems arising from the discussion of inflation versus growth were made more difficult when the United States reacted strongly against the sale by Bonn to Brazil of a $40 billion nuclear energy system, including a nuclear reprocessing plant. Washington viewed this sale as a dangerous move toward nuclear proliferation; Bonn complained that it was unreasonable commercial interference. Then the United States insisted upon the concurrence of the Allies before it introduced the neutron bomb. Bonn could not accept this, whereupon Carter shelved the entire issue, leaving Schmidt in an embarrassing situation within his own party and with the Soviets. In May 1979, NATO defense ministers met in Florida and adopted a proposal by the United States to develop a new Eurostrategic nuclear weapons package, including the 1000-mile-range Pershing II missile, development of an intermediate-range missile, and ground- or air-launched cruise missiles, as well as specific arms control incentives, such as reducing the number of nuclear artillery and air-delivered warheads in Europe. The Europeans were to develop a plan for deploying these weapons by December 1979. This goal was met, representing a major turning point for the Alliance. Nonetheless Bonn expected firmer leadership from the United States, especially of the SALT agreements, which include prohibition of the transfer of technology for cruise missiles until 1982. This the Germans view as discriminatory during a period when Soviet "gray area" weapons—SS-20 and Backfire bomber—will continue to be deployed.[203] The Germans are concerned, as well, that the senatorial amendments will weaken the presidency; the changing terms of reference and American priorities for SALT III. There is also a general apprehension about the long-stalled MBFR talks in Vienna on force reductions. Thus while the Bundeswehr is the strongest land force in Western Europe, the strengthening of the posture and the failure to achieve troop reductions has left Bonn more dependent than ever on the United States for its security.[204]

Thus, as the SALT ratification became an issue in the presidential campaign activities, many Europeans voiced mounting concern about the effectiveness of American leadership. The Carter administration was charged with indecisiveness and lack of authority which was the consequence of a profound fragmentation of the American political system, reinforced further by the style of the President himself. "This is not isolationism. Rather, it is uncertainty over America's role and leadership, and a reflection of the difficulty of sorting out truly vital interests from less essential ones in an unpredictable world."[205]

After Carter dismissed five Cabinet members in July 1979, a leading member of the Bundestag CDU opposition and an exponent of strong ties between the Federal Republic and the United States, Alois Mertes, publicly criticized the administration. Carter's zigzagging on major issues, he stated, and the personnel changes were alarming Europeans and endangering the life of the Alliance. "The belief in the American security guarantee for Europe does not only rest on power. It stands especially on the trust of Europeans in the political leaders, the capability and calculability of the American President. . . . Soviet policy is coming to be more effective toward the European allies of America—because it is more disciplined, competent and calculable than the one coming from Washington."[206]

Mertes' views closely parallel those long held, and only barely concealed, by Chancellor Helmut Schmidt. It was widely maintained during the summer of 1979 in Bonn that

Schmidt's personal animosity against Jimmy Carter for his alleged ineptitude, indecisiveness and lack of leadership was seeping beyond the Chancellory to the bureaucracies of the key ministries, especially the Ministry of Defense under Hans Apel. While communications between the two capitals remained friendly, a new tone of criticism had emerged. The Germans insisted on strong leadership and the Americans repeatedly answered that they were in "no win - no lose" situations. These new strains, the worst since the early Kennedy years, should be taken seriously, in light of German anxiety about the outcome of the 1980 elections in both countries.

German concern is underlined because the possible flagging in the future leadership of the United States coincides with increasing uncertainties about the stability of the international order. Only Germany and Japan could fill the possible political vacuum that may emerge on issues critical to other industrialized nations. But both are highly reluctant to increase their political roles and influence in international affairs, much less to deploy forces outside their national borders, for example to the Middle East, to protect vital interests. Thus, Bonn's problem, as Schmidt apparently perceives it, is to determine how much and what kind of support should be afforded an ailing American presidency and what new commitments to European stability should be enticed from the United States or endorsed in return, or what alternatives should now be explored to provide greater political flexibility, enhanced regional security, and reduced political and economic vulnerability. Experienced "Bonn hands," however, acknowledge that there are few options, especially if the FRG wants to maintain its present policy toward the GDR without making major concessions. Besides, ties with the United States, in general, are still positive, dynamic, and mutually beneficial.

Helmut Schmidt, himself, offered guidelines for West German development in his 30-year anniversary address of the founding of the Federal Republic.[207] The FRG can be characterized, after 30 years, as a state and society within which old ideas of progress, humanity, and justice are being tested at a time when old faces are disappearing. West German production workers, averaging more than $9 per hour, are the best paid of any large industrial country. In 1979 unemployment remained steady at 3.8 percent or 900,000; inflation has been held to 3.5 percent, and economic growth is forecast for 4 percent. Despite the comfort of these developments, Schmidt challenged the nation to find goals, other than just materialism and prosperity, for a new generation that was not traumatized by the Nazi era or the devastation that followed; to develop more self-confidence in its democracy, so that extremism on a minor scale does not produce overreaction; to handle carefully the emergence of West Germany as an increasingly important power—and not just in economic terms—in a world in which relationships are now somewhat different than they have been in the last 30 years.

CONCLUSIONS

There is no evidence of a fundamental shift in Bonn's international priorities, but there are indications that the FRG is intensifying its efforts to protect both flanks against disruptions from either East or West. Nor can major shifts in the policy of the GDR be expected either. Nonetheless, while there is no doubt that the sense of insecurity in the SED is a primary component in the limits of *Abgrenzung* and cooperation with Bonn exercised by the GDR, *Ostpolitik* should not be judged as a failure. There have been major improvements in the functional relations and personal contacts between the two sides.

It is difficult to assess the benefits accrued by each state. However, it is apparent that both have achieved their minimal goals: The GDR broke out of isolation and gained international recognition, without the customary manifestations of indigenous legitimacy. The FRG contributed to the improved well-being of the East Germans (despite the accompanying social tensions) without seriously impairing general international acceptance of the two states in one nation concept.

The internal reconciliation within the SPD (despite continuous jabs and challenges from its left wing) was the principal move toward launching and conducting a fruitful policy toward the East. Yet, the relatively conservative nature of the present coalition of the SPD and FRP under Helmut Schmidt, resulting mainly from domestic and international economic problems, plus new tensions with the GDR, has forced the SPD to administer a holding action by means of modestly stimulating and constraining policies. The overriding issue the SPD must deal with is how to preserve hope among the East Germans for a viable reform of the present situation. Failure to provide that hope now will serve to maintain the influence of the SED and the status quo, even though it has not achieved genuine legitimacy and could foreclose the prospects of improving the lot of the "other" Germans.

One unforeseen complication of *Ostpolitik* has been that it has diversified the social structures of the GDR, making them potentially both more fragile and brittle. This diversification suggests that new forms of political pluralism may be emerging in the GDR, which lie beyond Bonn's intended goals for *Ostpolitik*. Both governments' cautious reactions to indications of dissent since 1976 suggest a sensitivity by each about the potentially unpredictability of the new situation. It was this increasingly delicate atmosphere that prompted Helmut Schmidt to announce at the SPD Party Congress in December 1979 his intention to meet with Erich Honecker for the first time with the hope of restoring more amiable relations.

One conclusion is convincingly clear. There was no comprehensive program behind *Ostpolitik,* and no overall FRG plan for the future of inner-German affairs can be expected soon. There are only limited prospects for intergovernment negotiations on significant issues. Nongovernmental contacts could be marginally expanded, including sports, and cultural and professional exchanges. A marked increase in trade does not seem imminent, largely because of a decline in Western credits, supplies, and markets. It may be possible, however, to generate East German interest at the corporate level in new production ventures in both states, or in third countries. The prospects for providing joint service facilities in third countries, especially Eastern Europe, likewise may prove feasible. These suggestions seem to define the extent of new inner-German contacts in the near future.

East Germany's area of maneuver, nonetheless, is limited by numerous domestic and international constraints, the most important of which is the dominant presence of Soviet power that must be considered in all major policy decisions. The 1970s have been marked by a gradual relaxation of the division of Europe. The resulting increased East European and Soviet exposure to the West by the lowering of the barriers has not created major domestic crises, but it has had important effects on political and security matters. The Soviets clearly have not perceived that the lowering of the barriers as a series of political confidence-building steps to the same extent the West has. Indeed, Moscow most likely views some measures, such as CSCE, as destabilizing and potentially dangerous to its national interests. Such an interpretation partially explains Soviet intransigence at the European disarmament negotiations (MBFR), which has eroded earlier Western expectations that military disengagement would correspond with political improvements and accelerate normalization.

The stalemate in European arms reductions also has contributed heavily to the dampening of détente and the growth of interdependence. It has likewise accentuated the importance of superpower relations and SALT II and III. Providing solutions to the principal political problems, now linked to strategic weapons, is viewed as the most feasible means of remedying many grievances of other countries, particularly those of the two Germanys. While the Carter administration initially pledged not to link the solutions to problems of foreign policy, the Soviets have consistently and adroitly done so to meet their diplomatic needs. But this also works in reverse. Prior to the crisis in Afghanistan, Moscow correctly perceived that its influence in Asia and the Middle East was probably at the lowest ebb in over 25 years and was at the lowest point in Western Europe in over ten years. The interrelationship of the causes for these failures may be, but probably are not, offset by marginal gains recently made in Africa and Vietnam. (Political influence that is expected from arms transfers and military assistance far more often than not have proven illusory for Moscow, particularly in less-accessible countries.) More important, these setbacks have, in many cases, provided advantages for the United States which can gain influence more readily through technological development and modernization. The USSR has gained advantages only by means of tactical and strategic arms. However, Soviet foreign policy, based on arms, has had an inevitable negative impact on détente and super power relations. In the past, the West generally interpreted international stability as a direct function of the pursuit of the national interests of each super power while refraining from seeking unilateral advantages. More recently the achievement of stability has been viewed as the exercise of mutual constraints, controlled by incentives and reciprocity, while various military options are explored, from disarmament to the development of new weapons systems. This redefinition of the relations between super powers corresponds only slightly to the Soviet concept of peaceful coexistence: competition in ideology and values, cooperation in selected substantive areas, and the establishment and maintenance of a military force superior to those of all potential opponents. Such an interpretation of peaceful coexistence is likely to continue governing the perceptions and policies involving the statement between the super powers exacerbated by the Soviet conquest of Afghanistan.

As a corollary, the present Soviet interpretation of Socialist Internationalism, that is, the simultaneous expansion and contraction of constraints in the adoption of the Soviet model for socialist development, will likely dictate future Kremlin policy toward Eastern Europe. It will both reinforce the GDR's policy of *Abgrenzung* and permit a modest growth of inner-German interdependency, based on functional interactions. It could also possibly lead ultimately to a mutual inner-German understanding of the minimum terms for normality. This would require acknowledgement by the GDR side that it will not eventually gain advantages at Bonn's expense. On the FRG side, improvements in human rights would have to be endorsed as an end itself and not as a first step toward radical political changes and the establishment of common institutions. Normality in the inner-German context can only be predicated on mutual respect for divergent value systems—a task more difficult for East Berlin than for Bonn.

Socialist Democracy is not Social Democracy. It is based on the collective will as interpreted by the party, not upon individual interests, demands, or rights. Yet it need not be so oppressive. Socialism with a human face in East Germany requires closer identification of the party with the individual interests. Social mobilization and exhortation are no longer required, if the party becomes sensitive to social expectations. The GDR has been more reluctant than several other socialist states in experimenting with consultations with the public, workers' self-management, and decentralized authority and decision-making. Moves in such directions could increase stability and the SED legitimacy and thereby widen the scope of *Abgrenzung*. On its part, Bonn must convince its own constituency and East Berlin's that the best means for preserving East Germans' expectations for modification is to encourage successive doctrinal shifts in the SED, for example, by decentralizing without interfering in that process.

Such proposals are appropriate admonitions, but they should be viewed from the realistic perspective of the views the two German societies now hold on the German questions. Public attitudes are notoriously difficult to assess on such broad questions as what is Germanness. Indeed, they are sometimes frivolous or fickle. East German popular opinion about the FRG ranges from expressions of superiority (verging on contempt) to curiosity and even fascination among some youth. Applicants for exit visas often reject political and economic conditions in the GDR and not necessarily embracing West German ideological tenets. The FRG is often regarded as the lesser of two evils.

For West Germans the attraction of the GDR wore off surprisingly quickly. This disenchantment was due to relative economic deprivation between the two sides. Citizens of the Federal Republic hae become westernized as compared to the "proper Germanness" of the East Germans. They have split, as well, because of the historic cultural differences between the

Eastern and the Western German provinces, the marginal historical interest of many West Germans (until recently the West Germans have been highly politicized but not especially interested in their past). The result is that within each society there is no consensus about what "Germany" is, or should be, as a nationalistic concept, a political entity or as a societal function. A collective German self-image no longer exists. With the aid of 30 years of foreign military presence, *the Germans have finally divided themselves.* Reunification is no longer the central issue of the German problem. The partition is! Not in order to penetrate a state hypersensitive about its national self-image, but to facilitate those personal and professional contacts among those individuals who desire them. The partition also symbolically represents the division of Europe during the Cold War. While it is presently inconceivable for many West Gemans, the normalization of relations between East and West Germany in the middle term is likely to parallel that between Germany and Austria!

This is not an unhealthy state: While the Germans have divided themselves and are seeking new national self-images and identification, they still regard each other as kinsmen with an ambivalent sense of curiosity and indifference. Nonetheless, of the many cases of divided nations throughout the world, the Germans have been one of the most successful in solving some questions, ignoring others, and agreeing to disagree about still other issues. The century-old German problem is now no longer one of unification and consolidation, but that of creating individual national consciousness that is not mutually antagonistic but conducive to accommodation.

Annex A

List of Formal Agreements between the Federal Republic of Germany and the German Democratic Republic from 1949 to 1979*

1. Agreement on Interzonal Railway Traffic, 3 September 1949.
2. Agreement on Interzonal Autobus Traffic between the Unified Economic Zones and Soviet Occupation Zone, 4 October 1949.
3. Accord on Trade, the German Bank (DM-West) Currency Area and the German State Bank (DM-Ost) Currency Area (Berliner Accord), 20 August 1951, Renegotiated on 16 August 1960 and again on 6 June 1969, 95 Appendices.
4. Accord between the GDR Railways and the West German Travel Agency, 8 July 1954.
5. Supplementary Statement on Negotiations between the Representatives of the East German Railway and the West German Railway on Questions of Improving and Expanding Interzonal Traffic, 12 July 1954, Berlin.
6. Agreement on Damage Settlement between the German Insurance Company Berlin (East) as well as United Insurance Company of Greater Berlin (Ost) and the Association

---

*The actual texts of many of these agreements can be found in *Die Entwicklung der Beziehungen zwischen der Bundesrepublik Deutschland und der Deutschen Demokratischen Republik 1969–1976: Bericht und Dokumentation*, Bundesministerium für innerdeutsche Beziehungen, April 1977, plus periodic supplementary documents and special issues of the *Bulletin*.

of Liability, Accident and Traffic Insurance Corporations, 13 November 1958.

7. Protocol on Issuing of "Wall Passes" for West Berliners to Visit Relatives in East Berlin, the Capital of the GDR, during the period of 18 December 1963 to 5 January 1964, 17 December 1963, Appendices covering subsequent "Wall Pass" agreements.

8. Exchange of letters, Protocols and Agreements concerning the Reconstruction and Maintenance of the Autobahn Bridge at Hirschberg, 14 August 1964.

9. Protocol on the Controls for Cargoes Shipped to West Berlin and West Berlin Cargoes Shipped to the FRG over the East German Railways, including Storage and Transit at Border Crossings, 9 September 1964.

10. Protocol on the Extension of "Wall Passes," 24 September 1964, with Appendices.

11. Protocol on the Further Extension of "Wall Passes" for West Berliners to Visit Relatives in East Berlin, the Capital of the GDR, 25 November 1965, Appendices.

12. Protocol on the Further Extension of "Wall Passes" for West Berliners to Visit Relatives in East Berlin, the Capital of the GDR, 7 March 1966, Appendices.

13. Protocol on the Further Employment of "Wall Passes" for Urgent Family Affairs, 6 October 1968.

14. Agreement on Special Aspects of Trade between FRG Interzonal Trade Office and the GDR Ministry of Foreign Trade, 6 December 1968.

15. Agreement between the High Authority of West German Railways and East German Minister for Railway Service on the Reestablishment of Potash Transportation, 11 and 12 September 1968.

16. Agreement between the West German Ministry for Post and Telecommunications and the East German Ministry for Post and Telecommunications on Calculations and Settlement for Post and Telecommunication Services between the GDR and the FRG, 29 April 1970, Appendices.

17. Protocol on the Negotiations between a Delegation from

the West German Ministry of Post and Telecommunications and the Delegation from the East German Ministry of Post and Telecommunications, 30 September 1971.

18. Agreement on the Erection and Setting into Operation of a Radio Facility between the FRG and GDR, 30 September 1971.

19. Accord between the Government of the FRG and the Government of the GDR on the Transit of Civilian Persons and Freight Transit between the FRG and Berlin (West), 17 December 1971, Appendices, Exchange of Letters and Protocol Notes.

20. Agreement between the Senate (Berlin West) and the Government of the GDR on Improving the Conditions for Travel and Visits (to the GDR), 20 December 1971, Protocol Notes.

21. Agreement between the Senate and the GDR Government on the Regulation of the Question of Enclaves through Territorial Exchange, 20 December 1971, Protocol Notes.

22. Agreement between the FRG Ministry of Justice and the GDR Minister of Finance on the Settlement of Damages resulting from Motor Vehicle Accidents, 26 April 1972.

23. Agreement between the FRG and the GDR over Transportation Questions, 26 May 1972, 13 Appendices.

24. Protocol Notes on Medical and Health Care as well as Medical Transportation of Persons Normally Residing in Berlin (West), 12 June 1972.

25. Protocol concerning Inner-waterways Shipping through Berlin (Ost) with Transit Freight Documents, between the Financial Directorate, Berlin and the GDR Customs Authority, 13 July 1972.

26. Agreement between the Senate and the GDR Government on Inclusion of the Area of the Former Potsdamer Railway Station in the Agreement of 20 December 1971 on Enclaves, 21 July 1972, Protocol Notes.

27. Settlement between the West German Railways and the GDR Ministry for Transportation on Railway Border Traffic, 25 September 1972, Attachments.

28. Exchange of Letters between the Senate and the GDR Government concerning the Calculation of Lump Sum Payments of Travel Entrance Fees, 30 October 1972.

29. Agreement between the Senate and GDR Government on Disposal of Garbage from Berlin (West) in the GDR, 27 October 1972, 10 Appendices.

30. Treaty on the Basic Conditions for Relations between the FRG and the GDR, 21 December 1972.

31. Agreement between West German Travel Agency and the GDR Travel Agency for Tourist Travel, 4 January 1973.

32. Agreement between the West German Association for Liability and Accident Motor Vehicle Insurance and State Insurance of the GDR on the Settlement of Damages resulting from Traffic Accidents and the Financing of First Aid for Accident Victims, 10 May 1973.

33. Exchange of Letters concerning Leasing Terms for Storage Rooms for Garbage Delivered into the GDR, 1 June 1973.

34. Technical Discussions on Official Sealing of Railway Cars at the GDR Railway Terminals Conducted by Customs Authority, Hansa and GDR Railways, 2 July 1973.

35. Agreement between the FRG Government and the GDR Government on the Principles for the Extension and Maintenance of Border Waterworks, 20 September 1973.

36. Agreement between the FRG Government and the GDR Government on Principles for Damages Inflicted at the Border between the FRG and the GDR, 20 September 1973.

37. Agreement on Purchase and Delivery of Iron and Steel between the FRG Interzonal Trade Office and the GDR Ministry for Foreign Trade, 1 and 15 November 1974.

38. Agreement between the FRG Travel Agency and the GDR Travel Bureau for Tourist Travel, 21 January 1974.

39. Agreement on Purchase and Delivery of Machine Tools between the FRG Interzonal Trade Office and GDR Minister of Foreign Trade, 13 February 1974.

40. "Agreement in Principle" concerning Alternative Transportation Facilities in Southern Berlin, 21 February 1974.

41. Protocol between the Government of the FRG and GDR on the Establishment of Permanent Diplomatic Representation, 14 March 1974, Four Letters.
42. Aide Memoir concerning Basic Documents on the Reconstruction of Bordermarkers Resulting from the Territorial Exchanges Cited in Protocol, dated 20 December 1971, 9 April 1974.
43. Aide Memoire concerning Changes to Protocol, 12 June 1972, dealing with Medical Assistance to Residents of Berlin (West), 11 April 1974.
44. Agreement between the FRG Ministry of Finance and GDR Ministry of Finance on the Transfer of Alimony Payments, 25 April 1974.
45. Agreement between FRG Ministry of Finance and the GDR Ministry of Finance on Transfer of Personal Credits in Specified Cases, 25 April 1974.
46. Accord between the Governments of the FRG and GDR in the Area of Health and Disease, 25 April 1974, Seven Attachments.
47. Protocol on the Regulation of Relations between the National Sports Organizations, 8 May 1974.
48. Agreement between the Governments of the FRG and GDR on Fishing Rights in the East German Portion of the Lubeck Estuary, 29 June 1974, Six Protocol Notes.
49. Protocol Note Designing the GDR Coastal Borderline, 29 June 1974.
50. Protocol Note by the Border Commission on the Mining of the Brown Coal Reserves on both Sides of the Border between Harlike and Helmstedt, 3 July 1974.
51. Accord, Yearly Extension of the Agreement between the Travel Agencies on Tourist Travel in the FRG and GDR, 4 December 1974.
52. Exchange of Letters between the Senate and the GDR Foreign Ministry on the Disposal of Garbage from Berlin (West) in the GDR, 11 December 1974.
53. Agreement between the Senate and the GDR Ministry of Transportation on Treatment of Sewage from Berlin (West), 12 December 1974.

54. Agreement on the Upper Limits of FRG Trade Credits for 1975 between Interzonal Trade Office and the GDR Ministry of Foreign Trade, 10 January 1975.
55. Accord on the Combining of Accounts 1 and 2 of the Berliner Accord, 9 July 1975.
56. Agreement on the Restoration of the Berliner Accord which Regulates the Extension of Fixed Credits by West German and West Berlin Banks up to 1.1 Billion DM for Long-term Contracts in Areas Under the Berliner Accord.
57. Preliminary Accord Regulating Brown Coal Mining in the Border Area Helmstedt-Harbke between the Interzonal Trade Office and the GDR Ministry of Foreign Trade, 15 October 1975.
58. Exchange of Letters between the Senate and the GDR Foreign Ministry on Rescue Measures to be Taken in the Event of an Accident on the Sector-borders, 28 October 1975.
59. Accord on the Annual Extension of the Tourist Travel Agreement, 18 December 1975.
60. Announcement by the FRG calling for an Improvement in Berlin Transportation Conditions, 22 December 1975.
61. Annual Agreement for the Upper Levels of FRG Trade Credits, 14 January 1976.
62. Agreement between the Governments of the FRG and GDR on the Operation, Control and Maintenance of Drinking Waterworks for the City of Duberstadt which lies on GDR Territory, 3 February 1976, Three Border Commission Protocols.
63. Accord between the Governments of the FRG and GDR in the Area of Post and Telecommunications, 30 March 1976, Four Protocols.
64. Agreement between the Interzonal Trade Office and the GDR Ministry of Foreign Trade on the Mining of Brown Coal in the Border Area, Helmstedt/Harbke, 19 May 1976.
65. Aide Memoire extending Annual Tourist Travel and including Berlin (West) Residents under this Document, 20 December.

66. Agreement extending the Annual Sports Accord, 10 January 1977.
67. Exchange of Letters between FRG and GDR Ministries for Post and Telecommunication concerning Lump Sum Payments by the FRG for these Services, 1977-1982, 19 October 1977.
68. Agreement of the Construction of a Second Chamber at the Spandau Locks between the Senate and the GDR Minister of Transportation, 1 December 1977.
69. Exchange of Letters between GDR Minister of Transportation and the Chief of the FRG Permanent Representatives over Minor Construction Undertaking, 22 December 1977.
70. Agreegment on the Eckertal Dam and Ecker Water Delivery System, 3 May 1979.
71. Communiqué by the Federal Republic on the Results of the Negotiations with the DDR on Traffic Questions (including Exchanges of Letters on the Construction and Financial Responsibilities for the Berlin-Hamburg Autobahn, Application of the Transit Agreement, Construction and Financial Responsibilities for Transit Water Systems, Construction and Financial Responsibilities for the Teltow Canal, Future Improvements in Berlin Traffic and Financial Transfer Procedures), 17 November 1978.
72. Agreement of the Regulations for the Erection and Operation of a Highwater Retention Basin on the It_3, 29 November 1979.
73. Protocol Recognizing the Principle of Examination, Renewal Supplementation of the Border Demarcation and a Compilation all Previous Relevant Documents, 29 November 1979.

Annex B

West German Imports
in Inter-German Trade

ANNEX B

WEST GERMAN IMPORTS IN INTER-GERMAN TRADE [1]

	1956–60 [2]	1961–65 [2]	1966–70 [2]	1971	1972	1973
			Breakdown in %			
Total [3]	100	100	100	100	100	100
Raw Materials and Producer Goods [4]	57.7	51.0	30.9	34.6	33.3	38.2
Iron and Steel [6]	0.6	0.9	4.7	8.0	6.8	6.1
Mining Products	23.9	22.7	8.1	3.8	4.1	3.3
Mineral Oil Products [5]	18.3	14.3	2.9	3.9	5.1	10.2
Chemical Products [5]	9.4	7.8	8.3	8.0	8.2	9.4
Non-Ferrous Metals [7]	0.5	0.4	3.2	6.2	4.0	4.0
Investment Goods	10.5	10.5	13.6	13.6	11.5	9.7
Tool and Die Products [8]	7.5	5.9	5.8	5.9	4.5	3.5

Consumer Goods	18.6	22.0	29.4	31.5	32.9	28.7
Textiles	10.8	10.1	10.4	10.7	11.3	10.3
Clothing	2.1	4.8	8.3	8.5	9.2	7.4
Wood Products	0.7	1.6	4.2	5.1	5.4	4.7
Agricultural and Food Products 9	13.1	16.2	25.6	19.5	21.5	22.7
Grain	2.9	5.0	7.7	5.0	4.5	4.3
Livestock, Meat and Products	5.3	4.7	8.4	6.4	8.9	9.7
Sugar and Sugar Goods	3.0	3.7	3.7	2.4	2.5	2.3

	1956–60	1961–65	1966–70	1971	1972	1973
			in Million DM			
Total 3	877	989	1844	2499	2927	2998
Raw Materials and Producer Goods 4–5	462	560	956	1230	1483	1428
Iron and Steel 6	244	292	295	255	294	366
Chemical Products 6	118	166	392	482	670	693
Non–Ferrous Metals 7	15	30	168	313	249	130
Investment Goods	192	171	421	655	601	859
Tool and Die Products 8	108	110	303	534	437	643
Consumer Goods	70	72	153	211	351	315
Agricultural and Food Products 9	152	183	304	371	457	365
Fodder Products	0	26	124	188	228	168

	1956–60	1961–65	1966–70	1971	1972	1973
			Breakdown in %			
Total3	100	100	100	100	100	100
Raw Materials and Producer Goods 4–5	52.7	56.6	51.8	49.2	50.7	47.6
Iron and Steel 6	27.8	29.5	16.0	10.2	10.0	12.2
Chemical Products 6	13.5	16.8	21.3	19.3	22.9	23.1
Non-Ferrous Metals 7	1.7	3.0	9.1	12.5	8.5	4.3
Investment Goods	21.9	17.3	22.8	26.2	20.5	28.7
Tool and Die Products 8	12.3	11.1	16.4	21.4	14.9	21.4
Consumer Goods	8.0	7.3	8.3	8.4	12.0	10.5
Agricultural and Food Products 9	17.3	18.5	16.5	14.8	15.6	12.2
Fodder Products	0.0	2.6	6.7	7.5	7.8	5.6

ANNEX B (continued)

1. Including Berlin (West).
2. Five-year average.
3. Including goods that could not be classified and amount to about 1 percent of the purchases.
4. Including mining products.
5. Including synthetic products such as rubber and asbestos goods.
6. Including Foundry products such as products from molding and casting.
7. Including nonferrous half metal products and nonferrous metal castings.
8. Including office machines and equipment and facilities for electronic data processing.
9. Including semiluxury items and products from the fishing, forestry, and hunting industries.

Source: Bundesamt für Statistik, Wiesbaden, 1974.

THE DEVELOPMENT OF INTER-GERMAN COMMERCE

Increase in %

	Purchases	Shipments	Total Turnover	Balance
	in Mill. DM			
1950	415	330	745	− 85
1951-54[2]	281	261	542	− 19
1955	588	563	1151	− 25
1956	654	699	1353	46
1957	817	846	1663	29
1958	858	800	1659	− 58
1959	892	1079	1970	187
1960	1123	960	2082	−163
1961	941	873	1814	− 68
1962	914	853	1767	− 62
1963	1022	860	1882	−163
1964	1027	1151	2178	124
1965	1260	1206	2467	− 54
1966	1345	1625	2971	280
1967	1264	1483	2747	219
1968	1440	1422	2872	− 7
1969	1656	2272	3928	616
1970	1996	2416	4412	420
1971	2319	2499	4817	180
1972	2381	2927	5308	546
1973	2660	2998	5658	338
1974	3253	3671	6924	418
1975	3342	3922	7264	580
1976	3877	4269	8146	392
1977	3952	4341	8294	388

THE DEVELOPMENT OF INTER-GERMAN COMMERCE
(Continued) (2)

Compared to 1955

	Purchases	Shipments	Total Turnover
1950	.	.	.
1951-54[2]	.	.	.
1955	.	.	.
1956	11.2	24.3	17.6
1957	39.2	50.4	44.6
1958	46.0	42.3	44.2
1959	51.7	91.7	71.3
1960	90.9	70.5	81.0
1961	60.0	55.2	57.7
1962	55.5	51.6	53.6
1963	73.9	52.8	63.6
1964	74.8	104.6	89.3
1965	114.4	114.4	114.4
1966	128.8	188.9	158.2
1967	115.0	163.6	138.8
1968	144.9	154.6	149.6
1969	181.7	303.8	241.4
1979	239.5	339.3	283.4
1971	294.4	344.1	318.7
1972	304.9	419.9	361.2
1973	352.3	432.5	391.6
1974	453.2	552.1	501.6
1975	468.3	596.6	531.1
1976	559.3	658.2	607.7
1977	572.1	671.1	620.5

THE DEVELOPMENT OF INTER-GERMAN COMMERCE
(Continued) (3)

Compared to Previous Year

	Purchases	Shipments	Total Turnover
1950	.	.	.
1951-54[2]	.	.	.
1955	30.7	23.8	27.2
1956	11.2	24.3	17.6
1957	25.1	21.0	23.0
1958	5.0	- 5.4	- 0.3
1959	3.9	34.8	18.8
1960	26.2	-11.0	5.5
1961	-16.2	- 9.0	-12.9
1962	- 2.8	- 2.3	- 2.6
1963	11.8	0.8	6.5
1964	0.5	33.9	15.8
1965	22.7	4.8	13.2
1966	6.7	34.8	20.4
1967	- 6.1	- 8.8	- 7.5
1968	13.9	- 3.4	4.5
1969	15.1	58.6	36.8
1970	20.5	6.3	12.3
1971	16.2	3.4	10.4
1972	2.7	17.2	10.2
1973	11.7	2.4	6.6
1974	22.3	22.4	22.3
1975	2.7	6.8	4.9
1976	16.0	8.8	12.2
1977	1.9	1.6	1.8

1. Purchases, shipments of the Federal Republic
    from 1953 including Berlin-West.
2. Yearly average from 1955 including wage improve-
    ment, from 1956 including commerce in foreign
    currency.

Source: Bundesamt für Statistik: "Inter-Zonal Trade
    of the Federal Republic and West Berlin with the
    Currency Area of the DM-East"; from 1957: "
    "Commerce (or Commerce in Inter-Zonal Trade)
    between the Currency Area of the DM-West and the
    DM-East" and from 1969: "Commerce with the German
    Democratic Republic and Berlin (East)." Special
    Series F, Row 6.

Development of FRG Trade with the GDR since 1960

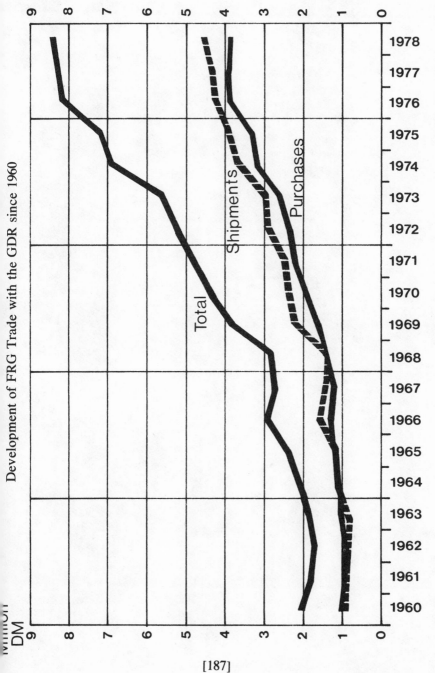

Source: *Warenverkehr mit der Deutschen Demokratischen Republik und Berlin (Ost)*, Fashseries 6, Statistisches Bundesamt, Wiesbaden.

[187]

Notes

1. There are a number of sound histories of the Federal Republic, e.g., see Peter H. Merkl, *The Origins of the West German Republic*, Oxford University Press, 1965, includes bibliography of relevant government and party documents; and Alfred Grosser, *Germany in Our Time*, Praeger, 1970, contains comprehensive bibliographic discussion. The most comprehensive bibliography up to 1972 is in William E. Griffith, *The Ostpolitik of the Federal Republic of Germany*, MIT Press, 1978.
2. Adenauer, Konrad, *Erinnerungen*, 4 vols., Deutsche Verlagsanstalt, 1968; Arnulf Baring, *Aussenpolitik in Adenauers Kanzlerdemokratie*, Oldenbourg, 1969; and Wolfram Hansrieder, *West German Foreign Policy*, 1949-1963, Stanford University Press, 1967.
3. Krisch, Henry, *German Politics under Soviet Occupation*, Columbia University Press, 1974, has published valuable new materials for which I am indebted.
4. Oppen, Beate Ruhm von, ed., *Documents on Germany under Occupation*, 1945-1954, Oxford University Press, 1955, pp. 29-39; Elmer Plischke, *History of the Allied High Commission for Germany*, US High Commission for Germany, 1951; Ingo von Münch, ed., *Dokumente des geteilten Deutschlands*, Kröner, 1968; J. Hohlfeld, ed., *Dokumente der deutschen Politik und Geschichte*, Wendler, 1952-55; and Thilo Vogelsang, *Das geteilte Deutschland*, DTV, 1966. For the Soviet documents see *Befehle dës Obersten Chefs der Sowjetischen Militärverwaltung in Deutschland*, SWA Verlag, 1946; Marshal Zhukov's Directive, "Richtlinien fur die Arbeit der deutschen Antifaschisten in dem von der Roten Armee besetzten Gebiet," *Beiträge zur Geschichte der deutschen Arbeiterbewegung*, No. 2, 1964, Krisch, op. cit.
5. Osterroth, F., and D. Schuster, *Chronik der deutschen Sozialdemokratie*, Dietz, 1963; Kurt R. Grossmann, *Emigration: Geschichte der Hitler-Flüchtlinge, 1933-1945*, Europ. Verlagsanstalt, 1970; and E. Matthias, ed., *Mit dem Gesicht nach Deutschland: Eine Dokumentation über die sozialdemokratische Emigration*, Droste, 1968.
6. Cited by Krisch, op. cit., pp. 43-44.
7. Kaden, Albrecht, *Einheit oder Freiheit: Die Wiedergründung der SPD 1945-1946*, Dietz, 1964; and Douglas A. Chalmers, *The Social-Democratic Party of Germany: From Working-Class Movement to Modern Political Party*, Yale University Press, 1964.
8. An unpublished speech cited in Krisch, op. cit., p. 59.

9. In an attempt to smooth the transition into the SED and to cement the union, the KPD published a definitive declaration by Anton Ackermann who again insisted that there was indeed a distinctive "special German Road to Socialism" which included parliamentary democracy. The main objectives of the new party were to advance democratic and socialist reconstruction through the effective use of state power not in opposing it through insurrection (Bolshevism). Peaceful transition to the full fruition of socialism was to be the slogan of the new party. Since the "coalition leftist forces" already controlled the instruments of state power under Soviet suzerainty, the goal of "correct" transition to socialism was an incentive for socialists to accept full participation in the SED. "Gibt es einen besonderen deutschen Weg zum Sozialismus." *Einheit*, February, 1946.

10. *Tass*, 26 April 1949. It should be noted that the best source materials for this period are found in U.S. Senate Committee on Foreign Relations, *Documents on Germany*, 1944-1961, G.P.O., 1961.

11. *Neues Deutschland*, 7 October 1949. The West German Parliamentary Council had commenced work on the Basic Law on 1 September 1948.

12. *New York Times*, 19 September 1950.

13. *Tass*, 22 October 1950.

14. *Neues Deutschland*, 3 December 1950.

15. Western occupation was ended by a subsequent Trilateral Protocol with the Federal Republic on the Termination of the Occupation Regime in the FRG, *United Nations Treaty Series*, vol. 333, p. 327.

16. *Neues Deutschland*, 1, 8 and 12 May 1952.

17. Ibid., 21 May 1952. (Indeed, Allied intelligence services had been tapping Soviet and East German telephone lines in East Berlin for some time.)

18. Soviet note 15 August 1953, *New York Times*, 16 August 1953.

19. *Frankfurter Allgemeine Zeitung*, 24 and 26 February 1954. The United States shared these sentiments about the burden borne by East Germans. After the June 1953 uprising, for which 62 persons were reportedly executed and 25,000 were imprisoned—many in Siberia—Eisenhower offered $15 million in foodstuffs. In three months 5 million food parcels were distributed in Berlin.

20. *Neues Deutschland*, 9 May 1955; also Sven Allard, *Russia and Austrian State Treaty: A Case Study of Soviet Policy in Europe*, Pennsylvania State University Press, 1970, and Hans-Peter Schwartz, *Vom Reich zur Bundesrepublik*, Luchterhand, Neuwied and Berlin, 1966.

21. Ibid., 19 January 1955.

22. During the next 15 years diplomatic reprisals were imposed on seven states for ties with the GDR.

23. Djilas, Milovan, *Conversations with Stalin*, Harcourt Brace, 1962; also *Wartime*, Harcourt, Brace, Jovanovich, 1977.

24. *Tass*, 11 November 1958.

25. Ibid., 11 December 1958.

26. Griffith, William E., *Albania and the Sino-Soviet Rift*, MIT Press, 1963.

27. Sorensen, Theodore C., *Kennedy*, Harper and Row, 1965, pp. 586-589; see also Arthur M. Schlesinger, Jr., *A Thousand Days: John F. Kennedy in the White House*, Houghton Mifflin, 1965; and U.S. Office of the Federal Register, *John F. Kennedy*, containing the public messages, speeches and statements of the President, January 20 to December 1961, G.P.O., 1962.
28. *Documents on Germany*, op. cit., pp. 652-55.
29. Schlesinger, op. cit., p. 381-85.
30. *Pravda*, 29 June 1961.
31. Ibid., 10 July 1961.
32. *U.S. Department of State Bulletin*, No. 45, 1961, p. 272.
33. See McNamara's elaboration of the Kennedy speech before the Senate Armed Forces Committee, 27 July 1961.
34. See *New York Times*, 23 July, 6 August 1961.
35. *Washington Post*, 11 August 1961.
36. Slusser, Robert M., *The Berlin Crisis of 1961*, Johns Hopkins University Press, 1973.
37. *Documents on International Affairs*, 1961, Royal Institute of International Affairs, Oxford University Press, 1964, pp. 343-45.
38. Ibid., pp. 341-42.
39. Slusser, op. cit., p. 136. See also John Mander, Berlin: *Hostage for the West*, Penguin, 1962. James L. Richardson, *Germany and the Atlantic Alliances*, Harvard University Press, 1966; Jack M. Slick, *The Berlin Crisis, 1958-1962*, University of Pennsylvania Press, 1971; Jean Edward Smith, *The Defense of Berlin*, Johns Hopkins University Press, 1963; Hans Speier, *Divided Berlin*, Praeger, 1961; Philip Windsor, *City on Leave*, Praeger, 1963; and Pierre Galante and Jack Miller, *The Berlin Wall*, Arthur Barker, 1965.
40. Sorensen, op. cit., p. 594-5.
41. See an interesting analysis of this conceptualization in Alexander L. George and Richard Smoke, *Deterrence in American Foreign Policy*, Columbia University Press, 1974, pp. 414-446.
42. Karl Kaiser lists three reasons for the policy change: (1) the Wall and the danger that the partition would become permanent; (2) Kennedy's détente policy and the threat that the division of Europe would be solved without settling the German problem; and (3) Moscow's overtures to de Gaulle, indicating the value of new policy alternatives—France was the first Western state to recognize the Oder-Neisse borders. *German Foreign Policy in Transition*, Oxford University Press, 1968. For further analysis see Bennett Kovrig, *The Myth of Liberation: East-Central Europe in U.S. Diplomacy and Politics since 1945*, Johns Hopkins University Press, 1973.
43. Jaspers, Karl, *Lebensfragen der deutschen Politik*, Piper, 1963.
44. The four parties are the Christian Democratic Union (CDU), the Bavarian-based Christian Social Union (CSU), the Liberal Free Democratic Party (FDP), and the Social Democratic Party (SPD).

45. Schröder, Gerhard, "Germany Looks at Eastern Europe," *Foreign Affairs*, October 1965.
46. *Die Bemühungen der deutschen Regierung und ihrer Verbündeten um die Einheit Deutschlands 1955-66*, Bundesrepublik Deutschland, Auswärtiges Amt, 1966.
47. Morgan, Roger, "The Scope of German Foreign Policy," *Yearbook of World Affairs, 1966*, Royal Institute of International Affairs, 1966.
48. Schmidt, Helmut, "Speech at Annual SPD Conference, 3 June 1966," *Tatsachen-Argumente*, 1966, p. 205.
49. *Parteitag der Sozialdemokratischen Partei Deutschland 1966: Protokoll der Verhandlungen 1966*. It should not be implied that attitudinal changes occurred only in the SPD. Gerhard Schröder and Rainer Barzel and others advanced ideas throughout 1966 on recognition of Eastern Europe, for example, as much to condition their party colleagues as to entice Eastern responses. But the ideological changes within the SPD were more profound and more noteworthy given its previous relationship with communism.
50. Government Declaration of 13 December, *Bulletin, FRG, Press and Information Office*, Bonn, 14 December 1966.
51. For documents of these events see *Germany and Eastern Europe Since 1945*, Keesing's Research Report No. 8, Charles Scribner's Sons, 1973.
52. Brzezinski, Zbigniew K., *Alternatives to Partition*, McGraw-Hill, p. 91; and "The Framework of East-West Reconciliation," *Foreign Relations*, January 1968.
53. Schaefer, Henry, *Comecon and the Politics of Integration*, Praeger, 1972.
54. For a comprehensive bibliography on domestic policy within the Soviet system see Lawrence L. Whetten, *Current Research in Comparative Communism: An Analysis and Bibliographic Guide*, Praeger, 1976.
55. *Scinteia* (Bucharest), 8 May 1966.
56. For a fuller account see chapters 3 and 4 in Lawrence L. Whetten, *Germany's Ostpolitik: Relations Between the Federal Republic and Warsaw Pact Countries*, Oxford University Press, 1971.
57. *New York Times*, 3, 10, and 22 May and 1, 12, and 16 June 1966.
58. "Interview with Foreign Minister Willy Brandt," *Münchener Merkur*, 25 July 1969.
59. Ceaucescu's Speech Before the Grand National Assembly, *Radio Bucharest*, 25 July 1967; and the Joint Communique on Foreign Minister Brandt's Visit, *Agerpes*, 21 August 1967; also Gerhard Wettig, *Community and Conflict in the Socialist Camp: The Soviet Union, East Germany and the German Problem*, St. Martins, *1975*.
60. Polemics on Rumania's move may be found in *Neues Deutschland*, 25 January, 3 February, 11 May, 12 June, 6 and 10 August 1967; *Scinteia*, 4 February, and *Radio Bucharest*, 25 July 1967; *Tass*, 8 February, *Radio Moscow*, 13 April and 8 August 1967; see also Peter Binder, *East Europe in Search of Security*, Johns Hopkins University Press, 1972.

61. Korbel, Joseph, *Détente in Europe*, Princeton University Press, 1972, p. 177.
62. As a summary statement see the Communique of the Karlovy Vary Conference. *Europa-Archiv*, 1967, Dokumente, p. D259, reproduced in *Survival*, July 1967.
63. *Izvestia*, 11 July 1968.
64. *The Policy of Renunciation of Force*, FRG Press and Information Office, Bonn, July 1968.
65. Ibid. See also Richard Löwenthal, ed., *Die Zweite Republik: 25 Jahre Bundesrepublik-Eine Bilanz*, Seewald, 1974.
66. *Pravda*, 18 September 1969.
67. *Frankfurter Allgemeine Zeitung*, 12 March: *der Spiegel*, 17 March; and *Frankfurter Rundschau*, 26 March 1969.
68. *Bonner Rundschau*, 26 March 1969; also Griffith, *Ostpolitik,,* op. cit.
69. *Frankfurter Allgemeine Zeitung*, 24 May 1969; and *Zycie Warszawy*, 1 April 1969.
70. *Die Welt*, 20 May 1969.
71. *Pravda*, 11 July 1969.
72. *Süddeutsche Zeitung*, 11 July 1969.
73. *Bulletin*, 23 September 1969.
74. Public opinion polls conducted by the Institute of Applied Social Science (Bad Godesberg), cited in *Bulletin*, 2 December 1969. The issues are slightly different but reflective of the current political climate.
75. *Bulletin and Supplement*, 4 November 1969.
76. Ibid., 18 November and 2 December; and official statements *Deutsche Presse-Agentur,* 8, 10, 11, and 17 November 1969.
77. *Zycie Literackie* (Cracow), 11 December 1969. See "East European Reactions to the June War: A Case Study in Soviet Foreign Policy Compartmentalization," in Lawrence L. Whetten, *Canal War: Four-Power Conflict in the Middle East*, MIT Press, 1974.
78. See *Pravda*, 6 December and Radio Moscow, 7 December; *Zycie Literackie* (Cracow), 11 and 14 December; *Rude Pravo*, 10 December; *Neues Deutschland*, 17 December; and *Radio Bucharest*, 14 December 1969.
79. *Bulletin*, Supplement, 20 January 1970.
80. *Bulletin*, 2 and 9 June and 9 July 1970.
81. *Europa Archiv, 25th Year, Dokumente*, pp. D396-399.
82. Excerpts of the Bundestag debate are in *Bulletin*, 22 September 1970.
83. *Europa Archiv*, 26th Year, 1971, pp. D25-6; and *Survival*, February 1971, pp. 69-71.
84. For the public debate see *Die Welt*, 4 and 12 December 1970; *Frankfurter Allgemeine Zeitung*, 23 November and 8 December 1970; *Rheinische Post*, 8 December 1970; and *Bulletin*, 8 and 15 December 1970.
85. *Neues Deutschland*, 17 December 1969.
86. See *Europa Archiv*, 1970, Dokument, pp. D190-3.
87. Ibid.; and *Neues Deutschland*, 10 and 12 January 1970.

88. *Neues Deutschland*, 15 and 20 January 1970.
89. *Bulletin*, 24 March 1970.
90. Ibid., 26 May 1970.
91. *Neues Deutschland*, 15 August 1970; see also *Bulletin*, 16 June, 14 and 17 July 1970.
92. Ibid., 10, 14 December 1970.
93. Interview in *Die Welt*, 28 January 1970.
94. Cieslar, Eva, et. al., *Der Streit um den Grundvertrag*, Olzog Verlag, 1973. This is a compilation of several hundred documents presented during the Constitutional Court litigation by the CSU contesting the legality of the *Grundvertrag*.
95. *Frankfurter Allgemeine Zeitung*, 15 July 1970.
96. Ibid., 19 September and 23 October 1970.
97. As an illustration of this dilemma, in February 1971, the GDR again offered to grant Wall passes for West Berliners but later withdrew the offer when the West Berlin Senat concluded that it could not negotiate specific accords without prior Four Power authorization.
98. The GDR claimed it was "forced" because of the continued violations of West Berlin's special status to exercise legal countermeasures (*Neues Deutschland*, 3 February 1971). The results were that between August 14, 1970 and March 31, 1971 Autobahn traffic was interfered with on at least ten occasions by East German guards and in one instance by Soviet blocking United States military convoys—for a total of 25 days of harassment with up to 30 hours of delays. There were also 21 instances of guards firing at refugees along the Wall. As the tempo increased during January and April 1971 the East Germans arrested 134 persons, detained 108 others for questioning, and denied 240 persons access to the Autobahns. Dennis L. Bark, *Agreement on Berlin*, American Enterprise Institute, 1974, p. 81.
99. The 2 million population of West Berlin is steadily declining: one quarter is over 65 and the birth rate is decreasing, while the movement to the FRG increases. It also has the third largest Turkish population behind Istanbul and Ankara.
100. Interview with Egon Franke in *Frankfurter Allgemeine Zeitung*, 14 February 1971.
101. *Zycie Warszawy*, 15 April, reprinted by *TASS* 16 April 1971, and *Frankfurter Allgemeine Zeitung*, 18 April 1971.
102. See *Dokumente zur Berlin-Frage 1944-1966;* and Detlef Merten in *Berlin als unternehmerische Aufgabe*, Gabler, 1971; and relevant papers published in *Deutschland Archiv*, during 1971.
103. *Tass*, 14 May 1971.
104. *Tass*, 25 May 1971.
105. *Neues Deutschland*, 16 June 1971.
106. *Current Foreign Policy; Berlin: the Four Power Agreement*, U.S. Dept. of State, Publication No. 8620, 1971. See also Marc Catudal, *The Berlin*

Agreement of 1971: Has It Worked? mimeo; and Dieter Mahncke, "The Berlin Agreement," *World Today*, December 1971. On the German side, *Bulletin*, 3 September 1971; and *Dokumentation Berlin: Die Vereinbarungen und das Abkommen*, West Berlin Senat, December 1971.

107. *New York Times*, 4 September 1971.

108. Bark, op. cit., p. 91. This interpretation is now widely contested.

109. ADN, 5 June 1972.

110. Doeking-Ress, *Staats-und völkerrechtliche Aspekte der Berlin-Regelung*, Bd XIII der Reihe, "Völkerrecht und Aussenpolitik," 1972. See also a legal brief by Dieter Blumenwitz on *The Diplomatic Representation of West Berliners by the Federal Republic*, 1975, mimeo.

111. In most cases West Berliners are afforded the legal protection of the Basic Law in processes in the FRG or West Berlin or nonsocialist countries. The issue is germane to litigation involving the Socialist states.

112. *Dokumentation Berlin*, op. cit.

113. Personal interviews conducted by the author in 1970's revealed a near consensus among West Berliners about the benefits they personally received and the positive implications for détente derived from the new access accord. Many visited East Berlin on nearly a weekly basis. But the former "skepticism-cum-optimism" has now changed to "skepticism-cum-pessimism" as détente appears to deteriorate.

114. The access routes include three air corridors, six railway lines, three highways, and two canals.

115. The "Transit Traffic" Agreement was signed on December 17, 1971 at the ministerial level, *Dokumentation Berlin*, op. cit. In related negotiations, an accord on communications was signed on 30 September by the FRG and the GDR on postal and telecommunications. Telecommunications between West Berlin and East Berlin had been cut by the GDR in May 1952 were to be restored and overall communications were to be improved between all three entities. Ibid.

116. Dokumentation Berlin: *Zur Anordnung der Regierung der DDR die Durchführung eines verbindlichen Mindestumtausches von Zahlungsmitteln vom 5 November 1973 betreffend*, East Berlin Press and Information Office, 1973.

117. Interview, *International Herald Tribune*, 14 July 1978.

118. Cieslar, op. cit.

119. The use of the treaty formula was also significant because of the weight attached to treaties under communist legal concepts. Only treaties can be incorporated into corpus of international law; indeed treaties are the primary basis for law. The full title of the Treaty is: Vertrag über die Grundlagen der Beziehungen zwischen der Bundesrepublik Deutschland und der Deutschen Demokratischen Republik. It is often cited as the *Grundlagenvertrag* or *Grundvertrag*.

120. The election results were a sharp increase for the SPD from 42.7 percent in 1969 to 45.9 and for the FDP from 5.6 to 8.4, and a drop of from 46.1

to 44.8 for the CDU/CSU. This unprecedented plurality for the SPD was interpreted by the overwhelming popularity of the *Ostpolitik*. See William Paterson, "The West German Election," *World Today*, December 1972.

121. Ceislar, op. cit.

122. See Brandt's interview in *Hessische Allgemeine Zeitung*, 4 October and Barzel's reply in the *Frankfurter Allgemeine Zeitung*, 13 November 1972. The official texts and accompanying documents, plus historical exchanges of correspondence on all the treaties see *Der Grundlagenvertrag*, Seminarmaterial des Gesamtdeutschen Instituts, August 1973; Antwort der Bundesregierung auf die Grosse Anfrage der Fraktion der CDU/CSU, betr. Deutschlandpolitik, Drucksache 7/2934, 6 December 1974; *Der Verkehrsvertrag*, Seminarmaterial des Gesamtdeutschen Instituts; *Die Berlin-Regelung*, ibid., with chronology of events related and official correspondence related to the Berlin problem; *Die Ostverträge*, ibid. For a conservative interpretation see *Partnerschaft mit dem Osten*, Lurz. 1976.

123. "Brief zur Deutschen Einheit," Cieslar, op. cit.

124. "Ostpolitik and the Present State and Future of Inner-German Contacts," in Lawrence L. Whetten, *Political Applications of Soviet Military Power*, Crane and Russak, 1976.

125. *Die Grenzkommission: Eine Dokumentation Über Grundlagem und Tätigkeit*. Bundesministerium für innerdeutsche Beziehungen, Bonn, February 1979. In announcing the protocol, Bundesminister für innerdeutsche Beziehungen, Egon Franke, praised the work of the commission but cautioned that progress through small steps was essential. Ibid.

126. "Mitteilung der Bundesregierung zum Ergebnis der Verhandlung mit der DDR zu Verkehrsfragen und zum Zahlungsverkehr," *Bulletin*, 17 November 1978.

127. *Statistische Angaben zum Verhältnis DDR-Bundesrepublik Deutschland*, BRD Innenministerium, August 1979.

128. A comprehensive government statement of its progress in fulfilling provisions of the Grundvertrag is, *Antwort der Bundesregierung auf die Grosse Anfrage der Abgeordneten und der Fraktion der CDU/CSU*, Drucksache 8/1553, 23 February 1978. For other interpretations see the criticisms and observations raised by the Bundestag Opposition in the most detailed criticism of the *Grundvertrag* since the Supreme Court hearing, *Antwort der Bundesregierung auf die Grosse Anfrage der Fraktion der CDU/CSU*, Drucksache 8/255, 4 April 1977.

129. Unless otherwise noted, the following tables have been compiled by the Federal Ministry for Inner-German Relations, August 1979 (cf.n.127)

130. *Bundesministerium für innerdeutsche Beziehungen*, op. cit.

131. Vincent, R. J., *Military Power and Political Influence, the USSR and Western Europe*, IISS, Adelphi Papers 119, p. 16.

132. Ambassador Kenneth Rush cited the perception of strength rather than enhanced military threats as the chief danger in United States troops' withdrawals frrom Europe (*USIS Bulletin*, 22 July 1973). See Vincent's classification of possible uses of Soviet power: the worst case would be

conquest of Europe; opportunism would involve a Hamburg grab; catalysis would require an invitation to participate in civil strife (Yugoslavia) and hot pursuit against insurrectionists (Czechslovakia); accretion or military presence would create a clash of interests (off-shore Norwegian oil rights), op. cit.

133. Brown, James F., "Détente and Soviet Policy in Eastern Europe," *Survey*, Summer 1974.
134. Windsor, Phillip, *Germany and the Management of Détente*, Chatto and Windus, 1971; also Thomas Wolfe, *Soviet Strategy at the Crossroads*, Rand Corp., 1964; and Michael McGuire, *Soviet Naval Developments*, Praeger, 1974.
135. Goldman, Marshall, "The Soviet Economy is not Immune," *Foreign Affairs*, Winter 1975-1976; also Elizabeth D. Valkenier, "New Trends in Soviet Economic Relations with the Third World," *World Politics*, April 1970; and Roger E. Kanet, *The Soviet Union and the Developing Nations*, Johns Hopkins University Press, 1974.
136. Szamuelz, Tiber, et. al., in entire issue of *Survey*, "Five Years After Khrushchev," Summer 1969.
137. In the ten years since 1966 the party leadership has remained remarkably stable; 81 percent of the living full members of the 1966 Central Committee retained their membership in 1971, and 89 percent of full members in 1971 were reelected in 1976. Jerry F. Hough, "The Brezhnev Era: The Man and the System," *Problems of Communism*, March-April 1976.
138. Soviet maneuvers are traced in Lawrence L. Whetten, *Great Power Behavior in the Arab-Israeli Conflict*, Adelphi Papers, Winter 1977, IISS, London.
139. Details of East European reactions are contained in Appendix A of Lawrence L. Whetten, *Canal War: Four Power Interactions in the Arab-Israeli Conflict*, MIT Press, 1974.
140. It should be noted that at the same time the USSR was also cautiously assertive. It violated the 1970 Suez Canal ceasefire, endorsed harassment of the Berlin autobahns, and attempted to construct a nuclear submarine base in Cuba.
141. Brezhnev raised the topic of the Middle East at San Clemente on June 22, but in such vague terms, it was not regarded as a warning. See Gromyko's UN General Assembly speech in September for further haziness.
142. The texts of all US-USSR summit documents, including the Basic Principles, are in Mason Willrich and John B. Rhinelander, eds., *SALT: The Moscow Agreements and Beyond*, Free Press 1974.
143. William E. Griffith pegged Soviet influence in the Arab world at roughly the 1955 level, "The Decline of Soviet Influence in the Middle East," in Lawrence L. Whetten, ed., *the Political Implications of Soviet Military Power*, op cit.
144. Kissinger, Henry A., Interview, *International Herald Tribune*, 6 December 1978. Some sources estimate that the figure may reach $80 billion by 1980.
145. The new tone was first set in "The Permanent Challenge to Peace," *USIS*

Bulletin, 4 February 1976. "Today, for the first time in our history, we face the stark reality that the challenge is unending; that there is no easy and surely no final answer; that there are no automatic solutions." Address by Henry A. Kissinger.

146. Mackintosh, Malcolm, "Moscow's Views of the Balance of Power, *The World Today*, March 1973.

147. Ludz, Peter C., "Ostpolitik and the Present State and Future Course of Inner-German Contacts," in *The Political Implications of Soviet Military Power*, op. cit.

148. Wohlstetter, Albert, "Is There a Strategic Arms Race?" *Foreign Policy*, Summer and Fall 1974; and Leon Sloss, "The US-Soviet Military Balance: Changing American Perceptions," in Lawrence L. Whetten, ed., *The Future of Soviet Military Power*, Crane and Russak, 1976.

149. See William F. Scott, *Soviet Sources of Military Doctrine and Strategy*, Crane and Russak, 1975; and General-Major E. S. Milovidov, ed., *Problems of Contemporary War*, G.P.O., 1972.

150. According to Helmut Sonnenfeldt, "The Soviet Union is only just beginning its truly 'imperial' phase. Its military forces have acquired intercontinental reach only fairly recently. Its capacity to influence events in remote areas is of relatively recent standing. And it is only just acquiring the habit of defining its interests on a global rather than a solely continental basis." Interview, *International Herald Tribune*, 26 January 1976.

151. Formally acknowledged in the November 1974 Vladivostok communique.

152. Khrushchev stated that peaceful coexistence was not a state of tranquility, but one of development and struggle. It presumes the revolutionary transformation of society that will accelerate the collapse of capitalism. Nikita S. Khrushchev, *For Victory in Peaceful Coexistence with Capitalism*, Progress Publishers, 1960.

153. Hassner, Pierre, *Europe in the Age of Negotiation*, The Washington Papers, No. 8, 1973.

154. According to Egon Bahr the *Grundvertrag* clarifies the elements of "noncomparability" of the German states which have ceased to be obstacles to the normal contribution the German peoples can make to stability. This kind of "abnormal normalization" is based on the mutual desire to cooperate, but also to maintain their respective distance. "German Ostpolitik and Superpower Relations," Speech delivered at Tutzing, FRG, 11 July 1973, reprinted in *Survival*, November-December, 1973.

155. Nerlich, Uwe and Johan J. Holst, eds., *Beyond Détente: European East-West Relationships in Atlantic Perspective*, Crane and Russak, 1977.

156. Nitze, Paul H., "Nuclear Strategy in an Era of Détente," *Foreign Affairs*, January 1976.

157. *New York Times*, 16 January 1980, and *International Herald Tribune*, 6 and 11 March 1978. See also Marshall Shulman's interview *Washington Post*, 16 January 1980.

158. Interviews conducted by the author in Moscow, March 1978. Whether Brezhnev's successor is a transitional figure, such as Kirilenko, or a dark horse candidate, it will be months, if not years, before he will have established the level of authority even the now weakened Brezhnev enjoys—the most decorated national figure since Stalin. It should not be overlooked that the soviets may be tempted to use the spectre of a period of less decisive leadership than Brezhnev's dynamic years to extract diplomatic concessions from the United States.

159. Interview, "The Real Paul Warnke," *The New Republic*, 26 March 1977. For an opposition perspective of that presented by the Carter Administration and the urgent need for "quick-fixes" for United States strategic forces, see William R. Van Cleave and W. Scott Thompson, *Strategic Options for the Early 1980's: What Can be Done?* Crane and Russak, 1979. See also the Senate SALT ratification hearings July-October 1979, and *New York Times*, 13 July 1979.

160. Hassner, Pierre, "Europe: Old Conflicts, New Rules," *Orbis*, Fall 1973.

161. See Kissinger's Press Statement in Moscow to this effect, *International Herald Tribune*, 22 January 1976.

162. Nerlich, Uwe, *Beyond Détente*, op. cit.

163. Ibid.

164. Zbigniew Brzezinski has commented about the options: "The alternative to détente is not war, but a variety of intermediate positions. Where there was no détente, there was no war either." Interview, *International Herald Tribune*, 26 January 1976.

165. Burton, John W., *World Society*, Cambridge University Press, 1972.

166. Legvold, Robert, "The Nature of Soviet Power," *Foreign Affairs*, October 1977.

167. The scenario which best describes how the Soviets could win a war and therefore which most concerns the West Europeans can be summarized as follows: the USSR achieves strategic surprise and launches a damage limiting first strike against strategic forces of the United States. There is no political or military provocation by the United States, although there had been a deterioration in relations between the United States and the Soviet Union and between East and West Europe. In the strike, 80 percent of the American ICBM force, 60 percent of the submarine-based SLBM force, and 60 percent of the bombers force are destroyed, plus other military targets, with the expenditure of 40 percent of Soviet ICBM's. Because of the radiation effects, command and control communications within the United States and NATO are seriously degraded. Damage assessment and reconnaissance of remaining Soviet strategic forces is impaired. In the meantime, Soviet SSBM's and bombers are dispersed. Under the circumstances, a retaliatory strike against the Soviet's military force would not warrant the expenditure of the remaining warheads; only a strike against Russian cities would be worth the expected retaliation against cities in the United States.

In a prewar exercise, over 100 Soviet attack submarines surge detected but unharmed into the North Atlantic. Moscow now announces a naval blockade and warns that it would attack any Allied shipping attempting to enter European waters. Europe is effectively isolated. The Soviet Union issues its terms for a peaceful settlement: The Soviet will not attack Western Europe if they are permitted the Finlandization of Western Europe. The United States must withdraw all military units, and dismantle strategic forces. Otherwise the United States would be forced to accept an escalation of "the war of nerves" in Europe and strikes against American targets.

This is clearly a "worst case" scenario that maximizes the Soviet advantage and minimizes that of NATO; yet, it emphasizes the possibility of paralyzing the United States and emasculating Western Europe.

168. Ritter, Klaus, *Two Germany's in Two Security Systems: Considering the Military Postures in the Context of Deterrence, Defense and Arms Control*, mimeo, September 1976.

169. Blumenwitz, Dieter, *The Atlantic Community in the Age of Détente*, mimeo, May 1976; also Robert O. Keohane and Joseph S. Ney, *Power and Interdependence*, Little and Brown, 1977.

170. For more detailed data consult the annual State of the Nation Reports. *Materialien zum Bericht zur Lage der Nation*, Bundesminister für innerdeutsche Beziehungen, 1971, 1972, and 1974.

171. Interview, *International Herald Tribune*, 22 October 1977.

172. Ibid., 15 March 1978.

173. Croan, Melvin, "A Quarter Century of the Two Germanies," *Survey*, Winter-Spring 1975, p. 80.

174. Ludz, Peter C., *The Changing Party Elite in East Germany*, MIT Press, 1972.

175. "Das Manifesto der Opposition," *Der Spiegel*, 2 and 9 January 1978.

176. For a different set of priorities see Fritz Ermath, *Internationalism, Security, and Legitimacy*, RAND, RM-5909-PR, March 1969.

177. Brown, James F., "Détente and Soviet Policy in Eastern Europe," *Survey*, Summer 1974, p. 46.

178. Grätz, Frank and Dieter Voigt, "The Influence of Material Stimuli on Social Structural Change in the Course of the Scientific-Technological Revolution in the GDR," *Deutschland Archiv*, Special Vol. 1976; and Karl H. Kahrs, "East Germany's New Economic System from the Point of View of Cybernetics," *East European Quarterly*, September 1972.

179. Wilczynski, Josef, *Socialist Economic Development and Reforms from Extensive to Intensive Growth Under Central Planning in the USSR, Eastern Europe and Yugoslavia*, Macmillian, 1972.

180. Ludz, Peter C., "Marxism and Systems Theory in a Bureaucratic Society," *Social Research*, No. 4, 1975.

181. For example see John M. Kramer, "The Energy Gap in Eastern Europe," *Survey*, Winter-Spring 1975.

182. Cited by Hartmut Zimmermann, "The GDR in the 1970's," *Problems of Communism*, March-April, 1978; see also *Materialien*, op cit., 1971, 1972, 1974; and Doris Cornelsen, et. al., *Handbuch der DDR Wirtschaft*, Rowohlt, 1977.

183. Ibid. See also Erich Honecker, *Die Rolle der Arbeiterklasse und ihrer Partei in der sozialistischen Gesellschaft*, Dietz Verlag, 1974, for a definitive statement of the Party's appraisal of societal needs.

184. For further empirical analyses of social structures as well as an amplification of the limited data base for studying social problems in the GDR see Peter C. Ludz, et. al., *DDR Handbuch*, Bundesministerium für innerdeutsche Beziehungen, Verlag Wissenschaft und Politik, 1975, and the revised 1979 edition.

185. Schierbaum, Hansjürgen. *Intra-German Relations*, Tuduv, 1979.

186. *Nordwest Zeitung*, 29 August 1977.

187. The first prominent victims of such a reformist movement were Professor Wolfgang Harich, jailed for ten years in 1957 and later Professor Robert Havemann who lost his university chair and has since been socially ostracized. After the Biermann expulsion Havemann was placed under house arrest.

188. The first victim of the expulsion tactic was ballad singer, Wolfgang Biermann, who was denied his East German citizenship in November 1976 while touring in his native West Germany (born in Hamburg). One hundred artists and performers who protested his expulsion were disciplined, ranging from party penalties, to arrest, to exile. He was followed by other leading artists and intellectuals, poetess Sarah Kirsch, poet Reiner Kunze, composer Tilo Medex, well known outside the GDR. Other lights included Nina Hagen, Katharina Thalbach, Ingolf Gorges, Uwe Schikora, Thomas Brasch, Eberhard Cohrs, Manfred Krug, Jurek Becker, Christian Kunert, Gerulf Pannach and Jürgen Fuchs—three of Biermann's closest friends.

    In May 1979 Stephan Heym, East Germany's most distinguished author was fined 9000 Ostmarks ($5000) allegedly for currency violations but apparently for publishing his book *Collin*, a psychological study of GDR secret police in the FRG. The GDR's most famous dissident, Professor Robert Havemann was released from two years house arrest and then fined in May 1979 10,000 Ostmarks for the same charges. In June Heym and eight of his supporters were expelled from the East German Authors Guild. Heym called the action a manifestation of "Prussian Stalinism." "A great silence will now erupt," he predicted," either from those imprisoned or those who do not want to be imprisoned which will speak louder than anything the Party might print." *Die Zeit*, 10 August 1979.

189. *Frankfurter Allgemeine Zeitung*, 27 August 1977. The authoritative Allensbach Institute of Demoscopie conducted a survey of 600 ethnic Germans who emigrated from Poland and the USSR between September 1976 and October 1977. Most, 49 percent considered they were living far

better, and another 40 percent only somewhat better and 4 percent said that their situation had deteriorated. Three percent stated that they would definitely have preferred to stay in the previous country. (This figure probably is confined largely to the elderly, but even so is not high. At least ten percent of the East German emigrates to the West return home.) *Ostkirchliche Informationen*, No. 4, 1979.

190. C. f., n. 45, and 175.

191. *Die Alternative: Zur Kritik des real existierenden Sozialismus*, Europäische Verlagsanstalt, 1977. For a critical review see *Die Zeit*, 4 November 1977.

192. Ibid., p. 400.

193. Ibid., p. 401.

194. According to numerous Czechoslovak emigrants interviewed by the author who insist on remaining unanimous, a sizeable segment (no figures given) of the Czechoslovak Army General Staff took the initiative in organizing a Pan-East European bloc of New National Communists. As planned, the bloc would jointly program and work for the advancement of Marxist socialism within the context of national priorities and requirements. There was no question of deviating from Marxism, only pursuing its perfection. The bloc would gradually adopt formal neutrality and military and political stance that would adequately reflect Soviet theater and strategic interests. The concept was essentially the creation of a socialist *cordon sanitaire* in Eastern Europe, regional Finlandization with equal consideration for Soviet and national interests. The transition was to be long-term and gradual. The Czechoslovaks broached the issue with military intelligentsia of other Pact members, including the USSR. Initial reactions were mixed, but not negative except in the GDR, because the plan did not adequately cope with the German problem and GDR independence. A second GDR objection was the issue of the level of Soviet troops stationed there and reentry rights to insure political stability in central Europe and the guarantee of the proper socialist "weight" in a possible settlement of the German problem. The Czechoslovaks avoid the issue, regarding it as the major regional obstacle to the promotion of their scheme.

The movement toward "New Communism" was to be initiated on the home front. At the September 1968 14th Party Congress, Dubcek was to be replaced by a political neutral and the hardliners, like Indra, were to be deposed. The creation of New Communism (Socialism with a Human Face) was intended to gain Soviet and East German confidence for achieving the eventual goal of a Finlandized Socialist East Europe. As early as May conservative elements within the Pact had voiced these reservations and had apparently already gained the dominating position. Events in Prague moved much faster and over a much broader spectrum than the military originators of the scheme intended, such as the publication in August of the proposed Party guidelines, guaranteeing the right of minority dissent, nullifying the concept of democratic centralism. Thus, the decision was made to denigrate the more conservative Czechoslovak military plan and "rescue" the hard line political faction. The closest to a formal statement of the proposal can be found in "Memorandum: The Formation and Codification of Czechoslovak National Interests in the Military Field." *Lidova Armia*, 2 July 1968.

195. On 25 July 1979, the GDR imposed harsh new restraints against Western journalists. In violation of the Helsinki Final Act, unauthorized contacts with East German citizens and unauthorized travel outside East Berlin were punishable by expulsion. Three journalists had been expelled during the previous two years, and the *Spiegel* office was permanently closed. Furthermore, passing unclassified information to foreign organizations was declared a treasonable crime for East Germans, punishable by 2 to twelve years in jail. Another law allows the regime to punish authors who publish materials in the West which "injure the Socialist way of life," with prison terms and fines up to 500,000 DM. In response Joachim Seyppel published a letter to SED chief ideologist, Kurt Hager comparing such practices to Stalinist and McCarthyite repression. "Is the state so weak it must fear a writer; can a writer be so strong as to unsettle a state?" *Frankfurter Rundschau*, May 3, 1979. Together they are the harshest laws enforced in Eastern Europe and are designed both to insulate East Germans against Western contacts and to provide the legal basis for firm action in the event of public unrest during the expected price rises for subsidized basic consumer necessities. See Peter Bender, "Der schwache deutsche Nachbar," *Die Zeit*, 10 August 1979.

196. Cited by Peter C. Ludz, *Legitimacy in a Divided Nation: The Case of East Germany*, mimeo, 22 April 1977. The seminal work on this issue is by Gebhard Schweigler, *National Consciousness in Divided Germany*, Sage, 1975.

197. Lipset, Seymour Martin, *Political Man: The Social Bases of Politics*, Doubleday, 1960.

198. Schweigler, Gebhard, *The Impact of Systemic Socio-Political Differences upon Current Forms of National Self-Images in Divided Nations*, Mimeo, 1979.

199. Ludz, Peter C., "Two Germanys in One World," in P. C. Ludz, *Dilemmas of the Atlantic Alliance*, Praeger, 1975; Dieter Blumenwitz *Fünf Jahre Grundvertragsurteil des Bundesverfassungsgerichts*, Carl Haymans Verlag, 1979.

200. Sinanian S., et. al., *Eastern Europe in the 1970's*, Praeger, 1972; and Jens Hacker, *Deutsche unter sich*. Seewald, 1977.

201. Janos, Andrew C., *Authoritarian Politics in Communist Europe: Uniformity and Diversity in One-Party States*, University of California Press, 1976. One manifestation of this insecurity is the extensive espionage program the GDR maintains in the FRG estimated at over 10,000 agents operating at any one time and at least one trial per day, resulting in periodic scandals at the highest levels of the Federal Republic. *International Herald Tribune*, 12 September 1978. The FRG has shown far less

interest in espionage; conversely the GDR operates a network that is greater in terms of total population than any other country, including the USSR.

202. One of the best presentations of all aspects of Germany's emerging role is in Viola Herms Drath, ed., *Germany in World Politics*. Cyrco Press, 1979.

203. Laurence Martin has observed, "Tolerating the Soviet Backfire bomber so long as it is not deployed in an anti-U.S. mode—that is so long as deployed against areas bordering the Warsaw Pact—is only the most explicit instance of going beyond merely neglecting threats to allies at SALT to actually diverting them in that direction, behavior of which Stalin suspected Chamberlain in 1939." *Washington Quarterly*, Winter 1979.

204. Griffith, William E., "The West-German-American Relationship: The Threat of Deterioration," *The Washington Quarterly*, Summer 1979, p. 86.

205. *Strategic Survey*, IISS, 1978, p. 9.

206. *Frankfurter Allgemeine Zeitung*, 27 July 1979. It called the statement "the most astonishing thing to come out of the opposition on foreign and security policy for quite a long time."

207. *Bulletin*, Bonn, 25 May 1979.

INDEX